the series on school refo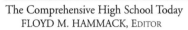

Patricia A. Wasley	Ann Lieberman
University of Washington	Carnegie Foundation for the
	Advancement of Teaching

SERIES EDITORS

(Continued)

the series on school reform, *continued*

The Comprehensive High School Today

EDITED BY

Floyd M. Hammack

Teachers College
Columbia University
New York and London

Published by Teachers College Press, 1234 Amsterdam Avenue, New York, NY 10027

Library of Congress Cataloging-in-Publication Data

The comprehensive high school today / edited by Floyd M. Hammack.
    p. cm. — (The series on school reform)
    Includes bibliographical references and index.
    ISBN 0-8077-4456-5 (cloth : alk. paper) — ISBN 0-8077-4455-7 (pbk. : alk. paper)
    1. High schools—United States—History. 2. Education, Secondary—Curricula—United States—History. 3. Educational change—United States—History. I. Hammack, Floyd M. II. Series.

    LA222.C555   2004
    373.73—dc22   2003070258

    ISBN 0-8077-4455-7 (paper)
    ISBN 0-8077-4456-5 (cloth)

Printed on acid-free paper

Manufactured in the United States of America

11 10 09 08 07 06 05 04   8 7 6 5 4 3 2 1

acadom - class, bks, teach, Hw.

Contents

Acknowledgments

This project would not have taken place without the support of a number of colleagues and institutions. I have benefited throughout my career from the active support of colleagues at New York University and especially the Steinhardt School of Education. My work has been supported by the School's Research Challenge Grant Award as well as by the good advice and suggestions of many friends. I would especially like to thank Dean Ellen Conliffe Lagemann, now of the Graduate School of Education at Harvard University. It was during her stay at New York University and her leadership of the Center for the Study of American Culture and Education that this project was launched. Interim Dean Thomas James, now at NYU, but soon off to the University of North Carolina, also provided encouragement. Lee Frissell, Director of Field Projects at the Steinhardt School of Education, was very helpful at the early stages of the project.

The support of the Spencer Foundation for a series of seminars was pivotal to the completion of the project. The papers that have become the chapters for this book were commissioned for the project with the Foundation's grant.

Christine Donis-Keller, my graduate assistant for the project, provided invaluable help, and it was a pleasure to work with her. Several participants in the seminars were particularly helpful to the evolving conception of the work. Betsey Useem of the Philadelphia Education Fund and Mary Erina Driscoll of New York University frequently provided excellent suggestions and advice.

Professor Mitchell Stevens, a colleague at New York University, read Chapter 1 and offered important suggestions, as did students in several of my classes.

At Teachers College Press, the editorial suggestions of Susan Liddicoat, Acquisitions Editor, and Dr. Jonas Soltis, a reviewer, significantly strengthened the manuscript. Series Editor Joseph McDonald, a New York University colleague and project participant as well as an author of one of the chapters in this book, deserves special thanks.

Finally, not a word I write gets by without the scrutiny of my wife, Nancy Walker, and her critical eye. She has touched everything I do, and this project is no exception. I am better for it. Increasingly, my children, Andrew and Philip, have added their part to my education. Their tolerance for and interest in my "Conant Project" has helped to sustain me. My mother, Dorothy Morgan Hammack, has always stimulated and encouraged me. It is to her that I owe the greatest thanks.

None of this, of course, absolves me of the responsibility for this work, but I do appreciate all of the help I have received.

Introduction

FLOYD M. HAMMACK

The work that produced the essays in this collection began with a conversation I had with Ellen Lagemann about the possibility of reconsidering James B. Conant's *The American High School Today*, written in 1959, more than 40 years after its publication. Widely influential in its time, the book and its praise for the comprehensive model of secondary education have become equally widely condemned. At least from the early 1980s, with the publication of *Horace's Compromise* (1984) by Theodore Sizer and other books (e.g., Boyer, 1983; Powell, Farrar, & Cohen, 1985) up to the recent Angus and Mirel book, *The Failed Promise of the American High School, 1890–1995* (1999), the dominant model of U.S. high schools has received little support from researchers or reformers. Marsh and Codding (1999) summarize this view by asserting: "it is time to abolish the comprehensive American high school" (p. viii).

Thus, in the span of 40 years, the comprehensive high school has gone from praise to condemnation. It seemed an opportune time to reconsider the idea of comprehensiveness in secondary education. The more we talked about the idea, the more resonant the idea for the project became for me. Secondary education developed in the United States differently than in Europe, and this difference was referred to by many as a representative example of U.S. success in expanding educational opportunity. Certainly Conant thought so. He made explicit reference to the dual secondary systems common in Europe and how their segregating effects limited opportunity. The single U.S. high school, offering a variety of programs under one roof, served all the youth of a community and helped forge bonds among them. In his view, the form of organization of high schools was not only a pedagogical issue, but a social and political one as well. I wondered whether newer forms of secondary school organization, especially smaller ones with a single academic program or emphasis, could serve the social and political purposes so explicit in the thoughts of the designers of the comprehensive high school. Fortunately, the Spencer Foundation was interested in the project, and provided support for seminar meetings and the development of a number of papers on the topic.

The idea for the project, therefore, was to reconsider the comprehensive high school 40 years after Conant's *The American High School Today.* Researchers who could shed light on the historical development of secondary education in the United States were commissioned to write papers, as were a number of practitioners of several prominent reform efforts. The latter were asked to think about their work in the context of the comprehensive high school, its educational as well as social and political purposes. These papers were read at meetings held at New York University between 1998 and 2000. Seminar members came from across the academic community and secondary school educators and administrators. Authors had the opportunity to revise their original work in light of the reactions and commentaries provided in the seminar meetings.

The focus of the papers selected to form this book concerns the notion of comprehensiveness in U.S. secondary education. The historical discussions trace its rise as an explicitly valued aspect of our secondary schools and the objectives it seemed to help the educational system realize. Each chapter considers Conant's ideas and questions the degree to which comprehensiveness has really been achieved, and what some of its consequences have been—the most obvious and controversial one today has to do with school size.

There is not a single point of view represented in these chapters, nor was it my intention that there should be one. Rather, given the almost uniformly negative views of the comprehensive high school in the last 20 years or so, the reconsideration of this form of high school organization was intended to reflect the variety of opinion that currently exists. Why has educational thought turned so negative toward the comprehensive high school? There are a number of reasons, as the following chapters detail, but we should keep in mind that in a number of communities, especially in suburban communities, small towns, and many rural areas, there are high levels of satisfaction with the existing high schools and scant motivation to change their fundamental structure.

At the same time, in many urban communities, the strong dissatisfaction with the performance of the local high schools is palpable. High rates of academic disengagement, failure, and dropout, and of violence and disorder, have led many observers to call for smaller and more focused schools. Because of large demographic shifts, many urban school districts now serve a largely poor and minority student clientele, who need educational credentials more than ever. Many of the critics argue that the effort to provide several curricular programs of high quality, one of the important dimensions of comprehensiveness, divides the attention of administrators and teachers such that none of the programs are well developed and maintained. The college preparatory curriculum usually dominates, but if a school's staff also tries to do a reasonable job of offering vocational programs and a useful general education curriculum, none of them will be particularly strong or effective, these critics assert.

I begin the collection with an essay that reviews the history of secondary education in the United States since the latter part of the 19th century. This period includes the development of the idea of comprehensiveness and the dramatic expansion of secondary education through the mid-20th century. The details of this history are well known, though the interpretation of the value of comprehensiveness, as I have noted above, is very much in dispute. The contours of these disputes are also described.

This review of the development of secondary education in the United States cannot, however, be seen in isolation from other developments in education, or in the wider society. In this light, my essay then proceeds to briefly examine how higher education has expanded in the post–World War II era and what consequences that expansion has had and is having on circumstances facing secondary education.

In Chapter 2 Joseph McDonald provides additional historical perspective and addresses what he terms the "core dilemma" of secondary education—how to meet the need to serve both the civic, public interests of the entire community and the private purposes of individuals, how, in other words, "to serve everyone and still give my child a competitive advantage." McDonald traces how several prominent educators conceived of secondary education along this axis and contrasts the views of Conant and Sizer.

In Chapter 3 John Rury, taking his lead from Conant's *Slums and Suburbs*, then addresses how other changes in U.S. society, particularly urban and suburban development, and demography, racial segregation and desegregation, the rise of a distinctive youth culture, and the evolution of the post–World War II economy have changed the landscape of secondary education. He focuses on how these changes have affected the ability of secondary education to realize the vision of comprehensive secondary schools and if the benefits of comprehensiveness that Conant articulated can be realized today.

Together these first three chapters are intended to frame the questions raised by the next set of chapters, whose intent is to examine some recent efforts at educational reform, given the general acceptance of the critique of comprehensiveness referred to above. These chapters provide another view of the problems facing secondary education today.

Because Conant emphasized the social and political role of schools as well as their academic role, I wanted a chapter to survey the literature on the ways comprehensive high schools provided an atmosphere for socialization that differed from schools of other types. Roger Shouse addresses just this question in Chapter 4. Explicitly reviewing the literature on school size, Shouse reminds us that the context in which instruction takes place sets certain parameters for the nature of what can be taught and learned. These limits may be hard to see and can sometimes be counterintuitive.

In Chapter 5 Jeannie Oakes and Amy Stuart Wells describe their research on detracking schools. In seeking to reverse comprehensiveness by eliminating curriculum differentiation, the efforts described in this chapter raise a number of critical issues about the social forces that create barriers to significant reform.

Mary Driscoll's Chapter 6 follows, surveying recent projects that connect schools to their communities. Developing the idea of a "sense of place," she applies it to Conant's legacy. She argues that the concept of place provides a perspective from which to better view the multiple purposes of the high school.

Finally, I conclude the collection with an assessment of the current status of the comprehensive school, both its myth and its reality.

As high school reform is a dynamic movement, new concerns continue to arise. Today, there are proposals for P–16 systems (Van de Water & Rainwater, 2001), in which secondary education is far more closely articulated with higher education. The problems of how to actually create a secondary system that offers a rigorous college preparatory education to an incredibly diverse population of students is something with which we are still struggling.

As the comprehensive high school was a child of rapidly expanding and diverse secondary enrollments at the turn of the 20th century, the new organizational forms with which we are experimenting today are the product of widely expanding and diverse postsecondary enrollments. What Conant could not imagine, nearly universal college enrollment, is close to reality, and the diverse curriculum of the comprehensive high school seems out of date today. How to fashion high schools that can graduate all or at least most of their students from a college preparatory curriculum may well be one of the defining educational policy questions of the 21st century.

REFERENCES

Angus, D. L., & Mirel, J. E. (1999). *The failed promise of the American high school, 1890–1995*. New York: Teachers College Press.

Boyer, E. L. (1983). *High school: A report of the Carnegie Foundation for the Advancement of Teaching*. New York: Harper & Row.

Conant, J. B. (1959). *The American high school today*. New York: McGraw-Hill.

Marsh, D., & Codding, J. (1999). *The new American high school*. Thousand Oaks, CA: Corwin Press.

Powell, A. G., Farrar, E., & Cohen, D. K. (1985). *The shopping mall high school: Winners and losers in the educational marketplace*. Boston: Houghton Mifflin.

Sizer, T. R. (1984). *Horace's Compromise: The Dilemma of the American High School*. Boston: Houghton Mifflin.

Van de Water, G., & Rainwater, T. (2001). *What is P–16 education? A primer for legislators—a practical introduction to the concept, language and policy issues of an integrated system of public education*. Denver: Education Commission of the States.

1

What Should Be Common and What Should Not?

James Bryant Conant and U.S. High School Reform

FLOYD M. HAMMACK

What should be common in the education of all youth and what should not? That question summarizes what has been one of the main issues for secondary education in the United States, as well as in other countries, during the 20th century. There is every reason to suspect that this issue will continue to confound educators and policymakers into the 21st century. As enrollments have soared and student bodies have become more diverse, the courses and programs of secondary schools have multiplied, and the curriculum is seen by some today as akin to the offerings of a shopping mall (Powell, Farrar, & Cohen, 1985). The 18th- and 19th-century vision of a common school, a school for all with a single curriculum for all, has long disappeared, and has been increasingly replaced by a mix of specialized schools for specific groups of students. Whether the comprehensive high school, providing a variety of programs for a cross-section of a community's students in one building, is a worthwhile idea today, or a practical one, is the question this book is intended to address.

The chapters collected here take up this question through an examination of the work of James Bryant Conant in relation to current efforts at reforming secondary education, especially as the reform concerns the structure of secondary education. In this chapter, I want to lay out the essential history of secondary school development in the United States over the last

125 years or so and place Conant's thinking in that context. Since secondary education is strongly influenced by and, in turn, influences higher education, I then take up an examination of the connections between these two sectors of our national educational system. Finally, I look at recent high school reform proposals and connect them with the idea of comprehensiveness and inquire about the continuing relevance of Conant's arguments in favor of it.

A SHORT HISTORY OF SECONDARY EDUCATION IN THE UNITED STATES

Up to the period after the Civil War, secondary education was largely limited to private academies, often closely associated with colleges, that served to prepare college aspirants for the rigors of the collegiate curriculum. According to Sizer (1964), for example, these schools often shadowed the college curriculum and taught Greek, Latin, mathematics, rhetoric, physics, and philosophy, and sometimes French. Few students actually graduated from these schools and entered college, but the purpose the schools served was clear. College preparation was their only mission. Of course, few young people entered college, and even fewer graduated. A high school diploma, let alone a college degree, was a marginal credential that offered little in return beyond access to a pulpit. Even then, many entered the clergy without college training. As early public high schools emerged, they too followed a college preparatory curriculum, though perhaps with less emphasis on Latin and Greek (Herbst, 1996; Reese, 1995). Dorn (1996) argues that two, contradictory forces were at work: the limited, selective nature of these academic institutions, with entrance usually by examination, and the demand by the public for wider access.

The solution to the tensions created by these conflicting aims developed in the latter half of the 19th century. Certainly by the 1880s, U.S. secondary schools began offering a more diverse curriculum. Commercial and mechanical courses of study were added, reflecting the interests of an increasingly growing and representative student body. However, this development alarmed many who thought the secondary curriculum should continue to be linked upward to the collegiate program of study. A result of this concern was the formation of the Committee of Ten for the study of secondary school studies (Krug, 1969). This group, chaired by Harvard president Charles Eliot, met for several years, and issued its final recommendations in 1894. The report confirmed that the curriculum of the secondary school should be centered on the collegiate disciplines and that all students would benefit from such study, whether headed to college or not.

Four courses of study were recommended, including the Classical, the Latin-Scientific, Modern Languages, and English. What distinguishes each is the balance of emphasis on Greek and Latin and on modern languages. The role of mathematics, history, and various scientific subjects is much the same across each of the four. The Committee strongly recommended against the differentiation of the curriculum into courses of study oriented to commercial or vocational courses in addition to one based on collegiate disciplines. As Krug (1969) summarizes, "a given subject should be taught the same way to all pupils regardless of their educational destinations" (p. 92).

Reaction to the report was immediate and frequently controversial. While the debates sometimes focused on the role of classical languages, especially Greek, the dominant debates came to center on the addition of noncollegiate subjects and courses of studies to the high school. Of course, the Committee of Ten report was in part a reaction to this differentiation, which was already strong by the 1880s, as Reese (1995) notes. Courses proliferated across the century's divide, especially as high school enrollments soared, nearly doubling every 10 years from 1890 to 1940 (National Center for Educational Statistics, Table 36, 2001). For example, in their classic book on *Middletown* the Lynds (1928) report that its high school had two courses of study in 1890 (Latin and English), but 12 by 1924, including many strictly vocational subjects such as applied electricity and bookkeeping.

Nearly 20 years after the Committee of Ten report was released, another study group was created by the same sponsoring groups that produced the original study, the National Educational Association and the Bureau of Education of the federal government. The Commission on the Reorganization of Secondary Education produced the *Cardinal Principles of Secondary Education* in 1918. In sharp contrast to the Committee of Ten report, the *Cardinal Principles* report asserted that the main objectives of secondary education also should include health, homemaking, vocational education, social-civic education, education for the wise use of leisure and ethics, and command of fundamental processes. This report explicitly envisioned universal secondary education, and encouraged most boys and girls to remain in school until 18, as full-time students, if possible. The Committee used the term "comprehensive high school" to name what it thought should be the dominant organizational form of secondary education, and described how such schools would develop differentiated curricular programs of study from which students could choose.

The *Cardinal Principles* report broadened the explicit purposes of high school to include community solidarity and citizenship.

> The school is the one agency that may be controlled definitely and consciously by our democracy for the purpose of unifying its people. In this process the secondary school must . . . [help] develop the common knowledge, common ideals, and common interests essential to American democracy. (1918, p. 17)

According to the authors of the report, this unifying purpose could be best served by a comprehensive high school. They asserted that the well-organized comprehensive school makes a differentiated education of greater value than can the specialized school, because it aids in a wise choice of curriculum, assists in readjustments when such are desirable, and provides for wider contacts essential to true success in every vocation. In more depth, the report recommended:

> Through friendships formed with pupils pursuing other curriculums and having vocational and educational goals widely different from their own, the pupils realize that the interests which they hold in common with others are, after all, far more important than the differences that would tend to make them antagonistic to others. Through school assemblies and organizations they acquire common ideas. Through group activities they secure training in cooperation. Through loyalty to a school which includes many groups they are prepared for loyalty to State and Nation. In short, the comprehensive school is the prototype of a democracy in which various groups must have a degree of self-consciousness as groups and yet be federated into a larger whole through the recognition of common interests and ideals. Life in such a school is a natural and valuable preparation for life in a democracy. (p. 20)

In 1944, the Educational Policies Commission (1952), sponsored by the National Education Association and the American Association of School Administrators, issued an influential report on secondary education entitled *Education for All American Youth* that recommended compulsory attendance until age 18 or high school graduation. The report inaugurated what came to be known as the Life Adjustment movement, extending school services "so as to meet all the educational needs of youth" (p. 18). It also set the stage for the assumption that all students should graduate, and for Dorn (1996) created the norm against which "dropouts" emerged as a social problem.

Thus, the comprehensive high school became the dominant form of secondary education in the United States (Krug, 1969). In Clark's terms (1985), one consequence of this addition of multiple missions meant that the high school became primarily coupled downward to elementary education, not upward, as it had been, to higher education. With the expansion of enrollments and of mission, the majority of students enrolled in non-college-preparatory programs of study, and as Angus and Mirel (1999) show, increasingly in general education programs, not vocational ones. Faculty increasingly identified with their colleagues in elementary school positions, and less often with faculty in postsecondary positions. Their professional associations found less in common with those of higher education faculty, and seldom did faculty move from high school positions to post-secondary ones (Stocking, 1985).

Moreover, this form of inclusive secondary schooling for everyone was celebrated as uniquely American, and was often promoted overseas as a more democratic form of education (Kerckhoff, Fogelman, Crook, & Reeder, 1996; Pring & Walford, 1997). As David Labaree (1988) asserts, this form was popular and enduring because it was the product of both politics and markets: it offered universal access and differential individual payoff. The tension between these pressures was internally contained through a highly stratified curriculum tracking system, though one open to all. Reserving the more highly valued college preparation track for higher-achieving students protected the value of college preparation, while offering vocational and general educational curricula for those not going on to college.

For Conant, these ideas were so well understood that they were virtually taken for granted. Having lived through the Great Depression and World War II, Conant was sensitive to the need for U.S. society to have a unifying agency, and he agreed that the school, especially the comprehensive high school, served this purpose very well. At the same time, it offered limited access to the college preparatory curricula. Though critics such as Bestor (1953) and Rickover (1959), and others during the post-*Sputnik* era, lamented the lack of rigor and of standards in the comprehensive high school curriculum, especially in the non-college-preparatory tracks, it was not until the early 1980s that serious criticism began to undermine the consensus that the comprehensive high school was among the greatest American achievements (National Commission on Excellence in Education, 1983).

THE AMERICAN HIGH SCHOOL TODAY:
A FIRST REPORT TO INTERESTED CITIZENS

Conant began his 1959 book with comparative history, briefly tracing the expansion of secondary education in the United States. He related this growth to the development of higher education, and throughout the discussion compared these patterns with those of European high schools and universities. In particular, Conant asserted that what set the United States apart from European countries was our commitment to equality, initially the political equality Jefferson championed, but later, as a result of the frontier, the concept widened to include economic opportunity through such programs as homesteading. By the late 19th century, for Americans, "equality became, above all, equality of opportunity—an equal start in a competitive struggle" (1959, p. 5).

By 1900, Conant argues, "the power of the twin ideals of equality of opportunity and equality of status" had led the American people to "believe that more education provided the means by which these ideals were to be realized" (1959, p. 7). As a result, along with institutional expansion among colleges and a declining need for child labor, especially in the rapidly expanding urban areas, enrollments in secondary schools expanded greatly. He cites the proportion of 17-year-olds enrolled in school, from 35% in 1910 to more than 70% at the time of his book, 1959. During the same period, the percentage of youth attending college jumped from 4% to 35%.

Having spent time in Germany after World War II as a high U.S. official, Conant was well aware of the forms of education in Europe and often mentioned how they contrasted with the United States. He was unfavorably impressed that in Europe, by contrast, common schools either never really existed or concluded at elementary levels, when adolescents were sorted, often on the basis of a national examination, and sent off to entirely different schools depending on the outcome of their examination. Some of these secondary schools led immediately to apprenticeship or other forms of employment, while the most prestigious, and smallest, segment prepared students for the university entrance examinations. Secondary schools that served all of a community's children simply did not exist. He notes that at the time of his book, "three-quarters or more of the youth go to work at fourteen or fifteen years of age" (p. 7).

The United States, responding to far more democratic forces, Conant asserted, evolved a secondary school where vocational and college preparatory education took place under the same roof. In an earlier essay, he wrote:

> One of the highly significant ideals of the American nation has been equality of opportunity. This ideal implies on the one hand a relatively fluid social structure changing from generation to generation, and on the other mutual respect between different vocational and economic groups, in short, a minimum of emphasis on class distinctions. It is of the utmost significance for our future that belief in this ideal be strengthened. (1945, p. 163)

He identified the comprehensive high school as an "instrument [that] can restore a high degree of fluidity to our social and economic life," lost with the end of the frontier. "Furthermore, education can inculcate the social and political ideals necessary for the development of a free and harmonious people operating an economic system based on private ownership and the profit motive but committed to the ideals of social justice." Illustrating the Cold War tensions of the time, Conant concluded that the nearer the United States came to providing equality of opportunity through education, and the more effectively the principles of American democracy were taught, "the more chance there is for personal liberty as we know it to continue in these United States" (1945, p. 163).

Another important aspect of Conant's thinking involved his sense that "academic talent" was a finite quantity among any cohort of youth. Though he cited, with approval, the expansion of secondary and collegiate enrollments, he thought that truly democratic schools would offer a variety of curricula, leading to different occupational careers. Students would be sorted among these courses and programs according to their performance, inclinations, and ambitions. The problem for our society was to provide the means to reduce the barriers to talent, wherever they were. When president of Harvard, Conant sponsored the founding of Harvard's National Scholarships, which sought to provide educational opportunities to the best and brightest students from across the country, not just from the preparatory schools of New England. For other students, he advocated expanded vocational education. He sought the elimination of "artificial barriers" to education, which he defined as geographical and financial. Embracing the efficiency and efficacy of the SAT and IQ tests, Conant believed about 15 to 20% of youth fell into the "academically talented" group who should prepare for college. He became very concerned about the process by which these talented youth were identified. Fearing that existing college selection processes overly benefited the children of the wealthy, his interest in college admissions testing grew.

In 1934 Conant was elected to the board of trustees of the Carnegie Foundation for the Advancement of Teaching, and in 1947 he became chairman of the board of the Educational Testing Service. Although he acknowledged the complaints of African Americans and others about possible discrimination in the tests, Conant thought that such assessments were more objective means of identification of talent and thus helped to remove the "artificial barriers" to equal opportunity for educational achievement. Combined with enhanced educational guidance, the identification of talent and the improved provision of educational options for all students as appropriate (e.g., academic and vocational) could be achieved.

Conant's faith in the objective measurement of "talent" or "ability" was firm (Lemann, 1999). Not all students were to be expected to have an interest in pursuing a college preparatory curriculum. However, the school had an explicit responsibility to keep open lines of mobility and to reduce the barriers to mobility. Moreover, the school had an explicit mission to ensure that students destined for different careers developed an appreciation for each other and felt a part of the school. The school was to offer opportunity for individual success, but was also obliged to encourage social solidarity. Much later, toward the end of his career, Conant (1970) stated, "The comprehensive high school has been defended on social and political grounds as an instrument of democracy, a way of mitigating the social stratification of society. Such has always been my argument" (p. 8).

"THE QUESTION TO BE ANSWERED"

In the section of the book named "The Question to Be Answered," Conant (1959) states,

> One can raise the question whether, under one roof and under the same management, it is possible for a school to fulfill satisfactorily three functions: Can a school at one and the same time provide a good general education for *all* the pupils as future citizens of a democracy, provide elective programs for the majority to develop useful skills, and educate adequately those with a talent for handling advanced academic subjects—particularly foreign languages and advanced mathematics? (p. 15)

This is the animating question of his book, and the one Conant sought to answer by visiting schools around the country with the support of the Carnegie Corporation of New York. In essence, his "Report" represents an attempt to assess whether the comprehensive high school really does a good job of the three tasks he had identified; whether, in fact, under one roof it is realistic to expect students to be well prepared for life and citizenship, for immediate employment, and for college. He developed criteria for assessing the degree to which each of these goals was being accomplished and sought quantitative and qualitative information relevant to judging the criteria. Using data from 22 highly comprehensive secondary schools studied in detail and 28 others he visited, he answers his question with a resounding "Yes." There were problems, especially the low level of academic expectations schools held for their "academically talented" students. In general, they were not asked to work "hard enough." He lamented the tendency for male students to emphasize math and science electives while their female counterparts were likely to avoid those subjects. He also was unhappy with the foreign language offerings of the schools studied, which provided too few options with a minimum of three years of study available.

Conant's report offers 21 recommendations to improve the comprehensive high school's ability to achieve all of the criteria he set forth. These recommendations cover a wide range of issues, but rest on the need for an adequate counseling system to create individual programs for all students that include a required set of studies in basic subjects, and classes that are grouped by ability. Other recommendations concern, for example, the provision of summer schools, special courses and programs for academically talented and highly gifted as well as very slow readers, the time devoted to English composition, and the pupil load for English teachers. These recommendations all concern issues relating to student diversity and to enhancing academic rigor. Overall, however, Conant strongly expressed the view that the comprehensive high school, as he defined it, was an ideal to which all of secondary education in the United States should strive.

HIGH SCHOOL REFORM TODAY
AND THE RELEVANCE OF CONANT

There seem to me to be three areas where our current reform efforts depart from Conant's vision of the comprehensive high school. The first regards the size of the school; the second, the use of ability grouping within courses (though he is explicitly against curriculum tracking); and third, the comprehensiveness itself, as opposed to a more specialized focus.

Conant was especially concerned that many high schools were too small to be truly comprehensive. He states:

> The prevalence of such schools—those with graduating classes of less than one hundred students—constitutes one of the serious obstacles to good secondary education throughout most of the United States. I believe that such schools are not in a position to provide a satisfactory education for any group of their students—the academically talented, the vocationally oriented, or the slow reader. (p. 80)

He details the sources of this opinion, stressing the lack of comprehensiveness in course offerings, especially for the academically talented at advanced levels and those seeking locally relevant vocational courses. Small schools are forced to include all students in the same classes, which "tends to affect adversely the tone of instruction and to encourage a lowering of grading standards" (p. 78). Conant thought there should be at least 100 students in each grade.

A core element of secondary school reform today is that comprehensive high schools are too big. Reformers insist that they need to be made smaller to encourage closer relationships between students and their teachers. There should be an environment characterized by a sense of "community" and one that is motivated by "personalism" (Lee, 2001; Raywid, 1998). Support seems to exist for the conclusion that while smaller schools benefit most students, they may benefit low-income and minority youth most (Howley, Strange, & Bickel, 2000). The current Federal Department of Education encourages reductions in school size, and some of the largest foundations are supporting plans to break up existing large schools into smaller academies (Steinberg & Allen, 2002; Zhao, 2002). It is worth observing, however, that according to the National Center for Educational Statistics (2001), the average U.S. high school's enrollment has grown from 684 to 785 students in the last 10 years. Efforts to reduce the size of high schools is an uphill battle as school districts struggle to provide capacity for a growing cohort of adolescents.

Conant acknowledged the existence of specialized academic high schools (often admitting students on the basis of an examination) and focused vocational high schools. He lists examples from New York City such as the Bronx High School of Science, the High School of Printing, and the High School of Performing Arts. Although he does not define these schools as anti-American, the implication of linking them with his discussion of European examples, juxtaposed with his depiction of the comprehensive high school as a uniquely American invention resulting from our commitment to democracy and to equality of opportunity, lends support for that supposition. While he does not support the closing of existing specialized schools, he does not support creating new ones. His research, he argues, supports the conclusion that comprehensive high schools can do the jobs of college preparation, vocational education, and citizenship/preparation for life in ways that are simply not possible in specialized schools.

Interestingly, Conant makes only rare, and then usually indirect, reference to the debates about the quality of American secondary education that arose during the late 1940s and increased in the 1950s, especially with the launching of *Sputnik*. As noted earlier, criticism of "life adjustment" education, and of the general lack of rigor of secondary education trumpeted by Bestor (1953), Rickover (1959), and others, received wide publicity at the time. Such criticisms have more recently been voiced by such scholars as Angus and Mirel (1999). Conant's defense of comprehensiveness can be seen as a response to their critique, while acknowledging that higher expectations need to be put in place for college-bound students. As noted earlier, Conant asserted that about 15 to 20% of an age cohort were "academically talented" and were to be academically challenged for college. The rest, he thought, should be well prepared for the vocational opportunities in the local community and should receive a solid general education. This required a differentiated curriculum as well as ability grouping among classes.

At the same time, Conant clearly saw the mission of creating and maintaining social solidarity among students and their families as best achieved through comprehensiveness. For him, specialized schools were antithetical to his view of the schools our democracy should develop. He recommends, for example, that senior social studies classes not be ability grouped. Rather, he asserts that classes in this course should be a cross-section of the school, and that the classes should be heterogeneously grouped.

> This course should develop not only an understanding of the American form of government and of the economic basis of our free society, but also mutual respect and understanding between different types of students. Current topics should be included; free discussion of controversial issues should be encouraged. (p. 75)

Combined with well-organized homerooms and various student activities, these classes can help produce citizens "who will be intelligent voters, stand firm under trying national conditions, and not to be beguiled by the oratory of those who appeal to special interests" (pp. 75–76). To Rickover and Bestor, among others, such ideas would sound softheaded and would not help the United States catch up to our international competitors.

In describing what he experienced on his visits, Conant said, "I was impressed with the success of the home-room in promoting an understanding between students of different vocational aims. One of the highly important objectives of a good comprehensive high school is surely developing a democratic spirit" (p. 27). In this respect, Conant was embracing a main tenant of the *Cardinal Principles of Secondary Education* report.

Consistent with his notions about the distribution of academic talent, and certainly reflecting his legacy as a university professor and as president of Harvard, Conant had a strong interest in the preparation of college-going youth. His sympathies toward this group of students are evident, and the curriculum for them was of particular interest. He wanted to assure that advanced courses in academic subjects were available and that individual classes in most subjects were homogeneously grouped. In the required subjects, and those electives selected by students with diverse prior educational achievements, he thought that "there should be at least three types of classes—one for the most able in the subject, another for the large group whose ability is about average, and another for the very slow readers who should be handled by special teachers" (p. 49).

Conant, however, did not encourage the creation of tracks—sets of courses hierarchically linked with specific purposes, such as college preparation—but rather emphasized individual programming of students into appropriate levels of classes. The individual focus on course programming also is reflected in the fact that his first recommendation for improving comprehensive high schools centered on its counseling system. He argued for a maximum ratio of 250 to 300 students for each counselor, which would afford the opportunity for counselors to get to know their students and parents. That every student should be offered an "individualized program" was the second recommendation. "There would be no classification of students according to clearly defined and labeled programs or tracks such as 'college preparatory,' 'vocational,' or 'commercial'" (p. 48). Student diversity should be accommodated in a fashion that encouraged mobility across the levels and kinds of curriculum the school offered. "It will turn out that many students of similar ability and vocational interests will have almost identical programs, but a student who has selected an academic sequence may shift to a vocational sequence and vice versa" (p. 46).

A common theme of the reform efforts dating from *A Nation at Risk* (National Commission on Excellence in Education, 1983) has been that the very idea of a comprehensive secondary school was flawed. The plans reformers have been promoting stress smaller size and greater curricular focus for all students within a school, thus deemphasizing internal differentiation and ability grouping. Joining this criticism is a somewhat different one, one that is based directly on the fact of comprehensiveness. These critics argue that in trying to offer curricula leading to different outcomes, comprehensive high schools dilute what may be possible in any of the curricula. That is, in trying to provide something for everybody, comprehensive high schools do none of it well. Sizer emphasized this notion when he called for "essential" schools (1984), and noted that "less is more."

These ideas have developed in an effort to enhance the academic performance of all students. Especially in urban centers, where the "achievement gap" between majority and minority students is very wide, reform has been motivated by the commitment to improve the performance of all students and improve the labor market options for all youth. For example, in their scathing critique of the comprehensive high school, Angus and Mirel (1999) write:

> Despite claims by educators that they were building "democracy's high school," the institutions they created were deeply undemocratic, providing only a small percentage of students with the opportunity to master the knowledge and skills that might lead to power and success in American society. Moreover, because educators increasingly sorted students by class, racial, and gender lines, the differentiated curriculum served to exacerbate rather than ameliorate the deepest divisions in American society. (p. 198)

Arguing for the primacy of an academic purpose (over the vocational, citizenship, and more general adult development purpose) of the mid-20th-century comprehensive high school, many observers today stress the need for all youth to achieve a level of academic skills necessary for college success. Whether citing the significant economic decline in the value of the high school diploma, the transformation of our labor markets in favor of more highly educated workers, or the untenable nature of the achievement gap in a democratic society, these writers all diverge dramatically from Conant's notion that perhaps 20% of high school students are "college material" (see, for example, Joftus, 2002; Martinez & Klopott, 2002). In fact, Rosenbaum (2001) now argues that we have developed a new educational norm: college for all.

Acknowledging how difficult it may be to achieve college-level preparation for all adolescents, however, some observers have encouraged the development of better systems for informing high school students of the demands of college-level courses. In his recent book *Beyond College for All: Career Paths for the Forgotten Half* (2001), Rosenbaum expresses the concern that as college for all becomes normative, other links to productive adult roles are not developed either by schools or students. Since many who begin college do not finish (less than 40% of those beginning the A.A. degree programs and less than 60% beginning B.A. programs eventually graduate [Choy, 2002]), their alternatives in the labor market are less than what they could have been.

> [It] is sad to see school systems dismantling vocational programs and bragging that they send large numbers of students to college but avoiding any mention of the large number of students who must take remedial courses in college and who drop out with no college credits. (p. 280)

In a similar vein, the final report of Stanford University's Bridge Project, *Betraying the College Dream: How Disconnected K–12 and Postsecondary Education Systems Undermine Student Aspirations* (Venezia, Kirst, & Antonio, 2003), found many high school students uninformed about the rigors of college work and poorly prepared by their high schools.

THE EXPANSION OF POSTSECONDARY ENROLLMENTS AND HIGH SCHOOL REFORM

The enormous expansion of higher education since 1960 (Dougherty, 1997; Trow, 1961, 1972) has dramatically affected the role of secondary education in the United States, and has had significant consequences for the comprehensive high school. More than 60% of high school graduates now enter some form of degree-granting higher education program. As enrollments swelled, so, too, did the variety of curricula available for college students. Following the pattern of the comprehensive high school in its evolution from a single-purpose institution, today few colleges have a majority of students majoring in traditional liberal arts subjects. Community colleges and most four-year colleges offer a wide array of vocationally oriented fields of study (Gilbert, 1995).

As I will briefly describe below, the growth of postsecondary education has clear consequences for high school reform. From its earlier role of providing a diverse education for all of a community's youth, the high school is increasingly being asked to bring all students to college preparatory standards. High school diplomas in many states are now contingent on students passing state exit tests, whatever their grades and course work show. Increasingly, these tests are aligned with college entrance standards (Van de Water & Krueger, 2002). It is now the responsibility of higher education, community colleges, and, to a lesser degree, comprehensive four-year colleges to offer the opportunity for educational advancement that Conant saw as the core mission of the comprehensive high school.

With this shift upward has come an evolution of the high schools' college preparation mission and its increasing stratification. For the highest-performing students, the line between high school and college is blurring. With admissions to selective colleges more competitive than ever and college costs soaring, middle-class parents and high-performing children are seeking high school programs that improve their chances of acceptance to "good" colleges, and that shorten the time to a degree.

The rise and spread of Advanced Placement (AP) courses, promising college credit for courses taken in high school, is one example of this trend. Building on work begun by the faculty of Kenyon College, who in 1951 proposed the creation of a way for high school seniors to begin working toward a liberal arts degree before college enrollment, and with the support of the Committee on Admission with Advanced Standing, funded by the Ford Foundation's Fund for the Advancement of Education, the system of examinations for college credit was begun in 1954 (diYanni, 2003). During the spring of 2002, about 1.5 million Advanced Placement exams were given to 900,000 students. Though the expansion of this program has been criticized (Committee on Programs for Advanced Study of Mathematics and Science in American High Schools Studies, 2002), it continues to grow, and some assert that it will become more popular than the SAT (Mathews, 2002). The pressure on high schools to offer Advance Placement courses is strong, and is often expressed by parents not only because they want their children challenged, but also because their time-to-degree can be substantially shortened. As tuition rises, this is not a trivial concern. At the same time, there is concern that some high schools, located in rural areas and in the inner cities, offer their students few opportunities to take AP classes (Mathews, 2002).

Another recent academic innovation in U.S. high schools is the International Baccalaureate (IB) (Gehring, 2001a). More than specific specialized courses, this program involves the entire curriculum of a school, or school-within-a-school. It combines a rigorous college preparation curriculum with an internationally oriented philosophy that appeals to many, especially in affluent communities. According to Mathews (2002), these programs are also growing fast.

So, too, are dual-enrollment programs (Bailey, Hughes, & Karp, 2003; Gehring, 2001b). Most often sponsored by community colleges, these programs offer high school students the opportunity to enroll in college-credit-bearing classes. The courses vary widely in where they meet, who teaches them, and whether the students are only high schoolers or are mixed with college students. Their popularity is growing, however, and is fueled by the effort to invigorate the "lost opportunity of the senior year" (Gehring, 2001b, p. 17).

Another indicator of the merging of secondary and postsecondary sectors can be found in the process known as "early admissions" and "early action" plans, in which students apply to college in the fall of the senior year and are informed of the results before the December holidays. While there are critics of the programs (Avery, Fairbanks, & Zeckhauser, 2003), what makes these programs interesting in this case is that they are another example of the blurring of the lines between high school and college.

Perhaps the best example of this blurring of boundaries is the Early College High Schools (Early College High School Initiative, n.d.) or the somewhat older schools that are part of the Middle College movement (Wechsler, 2001). Locating high schools on or close to college campuses, and offering their students access to the first two years of college and an Associate degree, these schools deliberately bridge the secondary and postsecondary educational sectors (Botstein, 1997). As with the other examples cited here, these schools are highly touted and expanding, and the initiatives backing them are well funded.

The process is strongest among the highest-performing students. It is at the schools serving these students that the largest AP enrollments occur; where the International Baccalaureate programs are most likely to be offered; and where dual-enrollment programs are made available. Colleges use early decision programs to select the highest-performing students. Mathews (2002) reports that 40% of U.S. high schools still do not not offer

AP classes, and though he does not provide the socioeconomic context of these schools, the strong likelihood is that most of the schools not offering AP classes serve poor and working-class neighborhoods. Thus, while the concerns of those berating comprehensive schools for withholding access to highly valued curricula are being addressed as high schools move toward college preparation for all, for the high achievers, graduation from high school now increasingly includes at least some college as well. In short, the advantages of the college-bound have not disappeared; these students are still ahead in the game. The escalating credential chase has increased educational requirements for all.

Somewhat ironically, the statewide exit tests, so prominent on the policy horizon, may turn out to be a countervailing force, urging an element of commonness across a diverse population of high schools. Efforts to democratize the offering of AP classes, often through distance learning opportunities, are growing as well. There is no doubt that these activities will increase the opportunity of rural and poor students to prepare for college. The problem is that their more advantaged peers are not standing still. Driven by their own sense of impending disadvantage, they and their parents seek college credit even earlier (Rimer, 2003).

CONCLUSIONS

The problem of providing a meaningful secondary education for all adolescents remains a vexing one. There are no easy solutions, given the enormous diversity of high school students and the divergent aims and purposes of secondary education in the United States. This review of the evolution of secondary education in the United States highlights some of the salient issues we face today.

The solution to adolescent education represented by the comprehensive high school seems inadequate from the vantage point of 2003. Yet, in our headlong drive to provide opportunity through education, perhaps all we have done is to raise the job entry point—where universal high school graduation was promoted in 1960, today we speak of universal college attendance, and preferably universal bachelor's degrees (Collins, 2002). While there can be little doubt that much can be gained by working toward reducing the achievement gap, the advantages of privileged youth will be very hard to overcome. As described above, the blending of secondary education with postsecondary education is an uneven process: the highest-achieving high school students now graduate from high school with college classroom experience and credits. The tension between the private benefits high schools can provide and their role in providing opportunities for educational advancement for the poor and minorities remain with us today as much as they did 100 ago.

Moreover, as we concentrate on the academic function of high schools, the citizenship mission that attempts to enhance social solidarity/integration across all segments of a community—the heterogeneous homeroom, the heterogeneously grouped senior social studies course emphasizing the problems of American democracy—are little spoken of by today's reformers. There are a few, such as Deborah Meier (1996), who do give voice to this mission, but they are outnumbered by those who define the school's democratic mission strictly in terms of affording greater individual opportunity and achievement or enhancing our nation's economic competitiveness.

To what degree, then, can today's secondary schools serve this integrating function? If they no longer enroll a cross-section of the children from the community, but rather concentrate on their academic purpose, are schools still able to be an "instrument of democracy"? If the ends of education are primarily identified as providing individuals with access to selective colleges or employment opportunity, how can the collective needs of the society be served? Or can the collective needs now only be served by addressing the individual social mobility function?

These questions highlight the dual, and perhaps contradictory, nature of the comprehensive ideal as articulated by James Conant (and highlighted by Labaree, 1990): The school was to serve both individual and collective ends. The individual interests served through providing equality of opportunity also were seen to strengthen the loyalty and commitment of students to the society providing them with educational opportunities. The following chapters explore the continuing relevance of Conant's work, and address many of the questions that arise concerning its usefulness for understanding whether and how education serves both individual and more societal purposes.

REFERENCES

Angus, D., & Mirel, J. (1999). *The failed promise of the American high school, 1890–1995.* New York: Teachers College Press.

Avery, A. F., Fairbanks, A., & Zeckhauser, R. (2003). *The early admissions game: Joining the elite.* Cambridge, MA: Harvard University Press.

Bailey, T., Hughes, K., & Karp, M. (2003). *Dual enrollment programs: Easing transitions from high school to college. CCRC Brief #17.* New York: Community College Research Center, Teachers College, Columbia University.

Bestor, A. [1953] (1985). *Educational wastelands: The retreat from learning in our public schools.* Chicago: University of Illinois Press

Botstein, L. (1997). *Jefferson's children: Education and the promise of American culture.* New York: Doubleday.

Choy, S. P. (2002). *Access and persistence: Findings from 10 years of longitudinal research on students.* Washington, D.C.: American Council on Education.

Clark, B. R. (1985). The high school and the university: What went wrong in America, I, II? *Phi Delta Kappan, 66,* 391–397; 472–475.

Collins, R. (2002). Credential inflation and the future of universities. In S. Brint (Ed.), *The future of the city of intellect: The changing American university* (pp. 23–46). Stanford, CA: Stanford University Press.

Commission on the Reorganization of Secondary Education. (1918). *Cardinal principles of secondary education.* Washington, D.C.: U.S. Bureau of Education, Bulletin No. 35.

Committee on Programs for Advanced Study of Mathematics and Science in American High Schools Studies. (2002). *Learning and understanding: Improving advanced study of mathematics and science in U.S. high schools.* Washington, D.C.: National Research Council.

Conant, J. B. (1945). Public education and the structure of American society: II. General education for American democracy. *Teachers College Record, 47* (3), 162–178.

Conant, J. B. (1959). *The American high school today: A first report to interested citizens.* New York: McGraw-Hill.

Conant, J. B. (1970). *My several lives: Memoirs of a social inventor.* New York: Harper & Row.

diYanni, B. (2003). the story of AP, the Advanced Placement program. Retrieved July 8, 2003, from the College Board, AP Web site: http://apcentral.collegeboard .com/members/article/1,3046,184–0–0–21502,00.html

Dorn, S. (1996). The changing mission of high schools. In S. Dorn, *Creating the dropout: An institutional and social history of school failure* (pp. 33–49). Westport, CT: Praeger.

Dougherty, K. (1997). Mass higher education: What is its impetus? What is its impact? *Teachers College Record, 99,* 66–72.

Early College High School Initiative. n.d. "Core principles." Available at: http:// www.earlycolleges.org/Downloads/CorePrinciples.pdf

Educational Policies Commission. (1952). *Education for all American youth.* Washington, DC: Author.

Gehring, J. (2001a). The international baccalaureate: "Cadillac" of college-prep programs. *Education Week, 20*(32), 19.

Gehring, J. (2001b). Dual-enrollment programs spreading. *Education Week, 20,* 32, 17–18.

Gilbert, J. (1995). The liberal arts college—Is it really an endangered species? *Change, 27,* 37–43.

Herbst, J. (1996). *The once and future school: Three hundred and fifty years of American secondary education.* New York: Routledge.

Howley, C., Strange, M., & Bickel, R. (2000). *Research about school size and school performance in impoverished communities.* ERIC Digest. Charleston, WV: ERIC Clearinghouse on Rural Education and Small Schools. (ED 448 968)

Joftus, S. (2002). *Every child a graduate: A framework for an excellent education for all middle and high school students.* Washington, D.C.: Alliance for Excellent Education.

Kerckhoff, A. C., Fogelman, K., Crook, D., & Reeder, D. (1996). *Going comprehensive in England and Wales: A study of uneven change.* London: Woburn Press.

Krug, E. A. (1969). *The shaping of the American high school: 1880–1920.* Madison, WI: University of Wisconsin Press.

Labaree, D. F. (1988). *The making of an American high school: The credentials market and Central High School of Philadelphia, 1938–1939.* New Haven: Yale University Press.

Labaree, D. F. (1990). From comprehensive high school to community college: Politics, markets, and the evolution of educational opportunity. In R. G. Corwin (Ed.), *Research in sociology of education and socialization* (pp. 203–240). Greenwich, CT: JAI Press.

Lee, V. E. (2001). *Restructuring high schools for equity and excellence: What works.* New York: Teachers College Press.

Lemann, N. (1999). *The big test: The secret history of the American meritocracy.* New York: Farrar, Straus and Giroux.

Lynd, R. S., & Lynd, H. M. (1928). *Middletown.* New York: Harcourt, Brace.

Martinez, M., & Klopott, S. (2002). *How is school reform tied to increasing college access and success for low-income and minority youth?* Washington, D.C.: Pathways to College Network Clearinghouse.

Mathews, J. (2002). Advanced placement. *Education Week, 21*(43), 68.

Meier, D. (1996). Supposing that . . . *Phi Delta Kappan 78*(4), 271–276.

National Center for Educational Statistics. (2001). *Digest of educational statistics, 2001.* Washington, D.C.: U.S. Department of Education.

National Commission on Excellence in Education. (1983). *A nation at risk.* Washington, D.C.: United States Department of Education.

National Education Association. (1894). *Report of the Committee of Ten on Secondary Schools.* New York: American Book Co.

Powell, A. G., Farrar, E., & Cohen, D. K. (1985). *The shopping mall high school: Winners and losers in the educational marketplace.* Boston: Houghton Mifflin.

Pring, R., & Walford, G. (Eds.). (1997). *Affirming the comprehensive ideal.* London: Falmer Press.

Raywid, M. A. (1998). Small school: A reform that works. *Educational Leadership, 55,* 4.

Reese, W. J. (1995). *The origins of the American high school.* New Haven: Yale University Press.

Rickover, H. G. (1959). *Education and freedom.* New York: Dutton

Rimer, S. (2003, March 9). Schools moving to curb wrangling over rankings: Valedictorian competition raises concerns. *New York Times,* 1, 20.

Rosenbaum, J. E. (2001). *Beyond college for all: Career paths for the forgotten half.* New York: Russell Sage Foundation.

Sizer, T. (1964). *The age of the academies.* New York: Teachers College Press.

Sizer, T. (1984). *Horace's compromise: The dilemma of the American high school.* Boston: Houghton Mifflin.

Steinberg, A., & Allen, L. (2002). *From large to small: Strategies for personalizing the high school.* Boston: Jobs for the Future. http://www.jff.org/jff/kc/library/0156

Stocking, C. (1985). The United States. In B. R. Clark (Ed.), *The school and the university: An international perspective* (pp. 239–263). Berkeley: University of California Press.

Trow, M. (1961). The second transformation of American secondary education. *International Journal of Comparative Sociology, 2*(2), 144–166.

Trow, M. (1972). *The expansion and transformation of higher education.* Morristown, N.J.: General Learning Press.

Van de Water, G., & Krueger, C. (2002). *P–16 Education.* Eugene: Clearinghouse on Educational Management, College of Education, University of Oregon. Brief #159.

Venezia, A., Kirst, M. W., & Antonio, A. L. (2003). *Betraying the college dream: How disconnected K–12 and postsecondary education systems undermine student aspirations.* Stanford, CA: The Stanford Institute for Higher Education Research.

Wechsler, H. S. (2001). *Access to success in the urban high school: The middle college movement.* New York: Teachers College Press.

Zhao, Y. (2002, April 10). $30 million grant to help small-school program. *The New York Times,* B7.

2

High School in the 21st Century

Managing the Core Dilemma

JOSEPH P. McDONALD

The American high school as we know it today—tuition-free and district-based, with four grades, and dividing time and space into major and minor courses—is about 150 years old. However, crucial features of the design—for example, "ability-leveled" subjects and a big, "comprehensive" curriculum—are barely 50 years old. These are the ones that James Conant advocated and helped establish in the middle of the 20th century.

Given its prevalence and our habituation to it, the high school may seem permanent. Yet 50 or 150 years is hardly the kind of longevity one can take as evidence of institutional permanence. In this chapter, I explore the possibility that the high school's dominance within secondary education may decline over the first few decades of the 21st century. If this occurs, it will be because Americans find a different way to manage the dilemma at the heart of secondary schooling, one that has occasioned 100 years of alternating efforts to tighten and then loosen the mission and curriculum of the high school.

In the second part of the chapter I explore this dilemma by means of a contrasting account of two of the high school's most important reformers. One is James Conant, and the other is Theodore Sizer. First, however, I must begin my argument at the beginning, since the argument is that American secondary education may in the 21st century revert to an old pattern.

ORIGINS

When the term *high school* was first used—in Boston in the 1820s—it doubtlessly sounded like a common adjective modifying a common noun. It did not acquire the institutional ring it has now until after the Civil War. Meanwhile, the institution itself did not become pervasive until the 1880s, and then only in the North. As William J. Reese (1995) puts it, "Americans throughout the early 1800's wrote approvingly of schools of a 'higher order'" (p. 34). But *high* was defined simply as anything beyond the rudiments. Thus, throughout the 19th century and even into the early 20th century, secondary education in the United States included multiple institutional designs, each one rising and falling in prominence, but also coexisting with others.

There were town-supported Latin grammar schools that emphasized the study of classical languages and texts, and prepared students for college. There were also small entrepreneurial schools that advertised in broadsides or newspapers, offering training in such practical subjects as writing or navigation or even gunnery. And there were tuition-supported academies and seminaries, thousands of them across the antebellum United States. Many offered some classical study, too, but most emphasized a practical curriculum with subjects appealing to their particular market. Among the subjects were bookkeeping, agriculture, needlework, surveying, military studies, and pedagogy. Coming and going according to fluctuations in the market, the academies varied widely in quality. Many, though not a majority, were subsidized by the states—for example, by land grants. Some were religious, though most were not. Some were single-sex, but many were coed. Most were boarding schools (Reese, 1995; Sizer, 1964a, 1964b). In addition to the town schools and the academies, there were also secondary departments of colleges, as well as colleges that combined what we would today call grades 11 through 14 (Gleason, 1995). There were also common schools that taught some number of older students the "higher branches," and town schools that reserved a top floor of their buildings for a "higher school."

Higher schooling proved so popular in the 19th century for the same reason that first the high school and then "higher education" proved so popular in the 20th—namely, changes in the economy. The new market economy reached even inland villages and farms in the early years of the 19th century, and advancing industrialization and labor organization disrupted established patterns of youth employment and apprenticeship (Labaree, 1988; Reese, 1995). As a result, the purpose of schooling shifted from the basic moral and political ones promoted by the state to the development of human capital—a purpose especially promoted by families wanting opportunities for their children (Cohen & Neufeld, 1981; Labaree, 1988).

This association between schooling and opportunity was consciously encouraged by elites who saw it as protection against class warfare—the latter being a continual danger amid the century's recurring panics and depressions, and in the aftermath of an appalling civil war (Reese, 1995). A consequence of the encouragement was rising demand for exactly the kind of secondary education the new high schools promised—modern, technical, occupationally oriented, available close to home, and free (Cohen & Neufeld, 1981; Reese, 1995). The last two of these features especially undercut the appeal of the academies. Although it would be well into the next century before working-class white youth as well as black and immigrant youth attended high schools in large numbers, nevertheless, by the end of the 19th century the high school had come to symbolize for many communities the new meritocratic ideal (and implicitly its social Darwinian underside). Often opulent in its architecture, the community's high school was ostensibly open to all the community's youth. Of course, its universality was pure myth, given its middle-class identity and the pervasive effects of racial segregation. Still, the myth took hold (Reese, 1995).

Meanwhile, the high school also represented the pinnacle of a rational, state-directed system of public education. The reformers who championed it hoped to replace what they regarded as the chaos of secondary schooling with an institution based on "age-graded classrooms, a unified curriculum, and hierarchical authority in the hands of men like themselves"(Reese, 1995, p. 21). Their aspiration was then still an emerging American ideal, rooted in Federalist and Whig ideology, but soon to flower in an amazing set of cultural, governmental, and economic transformations. It would become an enduring American ideal, though hardly an uncontested one—then or now.

Once established, the high school quickly changed its status from reform's solution to its problem. Having imported curricula from the academies and in many cases having absorbed the academies themselves, most high schools seemed to late-19th-century reformers as untidy as the academies had seemed to earlier reformers (Reese, 1995). Moreover, high schools marketed themselves to more and more youth as the century progressed, as if to justify their founding myth and also to placate taxpayers uncertain yet about whether their particular high school was worth its high cost. In the process, they made their curricula resemble what David Cohen calls "a species of academic jungle creeper, spreading thickly and quickly in many directions at once"(Powell, Farrar, & Cohen, 1985, p. 240).

In 1892, the National Education Association (NEA) appointed a group of influential educators to attempt some tidying up. This Committee of Ten, chaired by President Charles W. Eliot of Harvard, issued its report the next year (Krug, 1964; Sizer, 1964b). Some of its prescriptions took hold. Although the classicists fought back furiously, Eliot's dictum that physics was easily worth as much as Latin eventually prevailed (Powell et al., 1985). Moreover, his prescription of what he called the five curricular "main lines"—courses in English, mathematics, science, history, and foreign languages, to be packaged into classes lasting a little less than an hour a day—set the standard and the schedule of the high school for the next 100-plus years (Sizer, 1986). On the other hand, the Committee's admonition to maintain a strong intellectual focus in all high school courses for all students—in effect, to eliminate the nonacademic tracks—was largely ignored (Krug, 1964; Powell et al., 1985; Sizer, 1964b). It was not just because it ran into opposition from a coalition of psychologists and others with "modern" ideas about the social and developmental needs of youth, but also because it did not suit the employment market, which was deeply affected in the next decades by massive industrialization, immigration, and urbanization.

Influenced by these developments, the next high school reform of the century, also sponsored by the NEA and announced in a widely influential report, aimed to loosen rather than tighten the high school's mission and curriculum. The *Cardinal Principles of Education* (U.S. Bureau of Education, 1918) deemphasized academics and framed a mission for the high school that paid at least as much attention to things like health, leisure, citizenship, and "worthy home-membership." Its impact was compatible with that of the new technology of intelligence testing, which promised an efficient sorting out of those students for whom worthy home-membership ought to matter more than algebra. It was compatible, too, with the rise of the "extra-curriculum" of sports and clubs. It later accommodated the "life adjustment" movement also—influential by the late 1940s and well beyond—which suggested that personal needs rather than vocational aims should drive the curriculum (Powell et al., 1985).

Mostly because there were no jobs to lure them elsewhere, youth flocked to the high schools in the 1930s. Moreover, a sharply climbing number of them also stayed long enough to graduate (Powell et al., 1985). Meanwhile, the high school as an institution managed to fend off competition from New Deal educational programs for youth that might well have threatened its universality (Krug, 1972). The result is that high school became after 1930 a genuinely mass institution, though one that harbored a deep dilemma related to universality.

In their seminal 1981 essay, David Cohen and Barbara Neufeld identify the poles of this dilemma as the high school's promise of social equality, on the one hand, and its promise of individual distinction on the other.

Putting the dilemma in somewhat different terms, one might say that it involves the competition between, on the one hand, the school's public purpose—whether to instill republican virtue, keep youth out of the job market and off the streets, or educate workers for a new economy; and, on the other hand, the private interest that keeps students coming—namely to gain economic and social advantage. However one frames it, the dilemma is felt by the parent who wonders how the high school can possibly serve everybody, yet still give his or her child a competitive edge. The child feels it, too, as he or she struggles to maintain balance between the enormous social imposition of the high school—with its assembly-line structure and fierce peer pressure—and the drive to be an autonomous person and to have and express a unique identity.

For its part, the high school, and the whole apparatus of policy in which it is embedded, struggles to manage this core dilemma. How can students be both equal here and also distinct? Is the public purpose served by outcomes only, or by mere opportunity—as in everybody had a chance to gain real benefits, but only some did? Is the private interest served by status, or by attention? That is, is it spelled out in class rank and social standing, or in the benefits of being known well and cared for?

To understand this core dilemma and the long role that it has played in high school reform, it helps to compare and contrast the ideas of two 20th-century reformers who focused their efforts squarely on it. One began his reform work toward the end of the 1950s, when because of *Sputnik* the Cardinal Principles suddenly seemed a security threat. In those days, tightening up the high school's mission and focus seemed an appropriate response. The other reformer began his reform work toward the end of the 1970s, following a decade in which the high school had tried to adjust to the civil rights movement and also to the rise of a powerful youth culture, in the process loosening mission and curriculum once again.

TALE OF TWO REFORMERS

As it happens, both these reformers came from Harvard. James Conant had been the young chair of the chemistry department there, then took over as president of the university in 1933. Theodore Sizer was promoted at a young age from assistant professor to dean of Harvard's Graduate School of Education in 1964. In plotting their respective high school reform strategies, both men consciously emulated the earlier Harvard official turned high school reformer Charles W. Eliot. The Harvard connection lent the efforts of all three reformers an extrapolitical character, gave it intellectual appeal, and provided conservative cover for what was in reality a radical outlook.

It is important to note, however, that neither Conant nor Sizer became a high school reformer straight from Harvard. What each did in between came to matter later. Conant left Harvard in 1953 to become U.S. High Commissioner in occupied Germany, while Sizer left Harvard in 1972 to become headmaster of Phillips Academy, Andover. The difference in career trajectories—with years spent in nation-rebuilding versus years spent in tending a particular school's culture—may account for a crucial difference in how they came to view the core dilemma of the high school. As Sizer wrote in the preface to *Horace's Hope* (1996):

> In 1981, I had just completed nine years as a high school principal and history teacher, and I was intensely aware of the nature and craft of school-keeping, the incessant, fascinating dailiness of that craft, and the wonderful specialness of adolescents. . . . The angle from which one views schools matters. (p. xii)

Conant, by contrast, inveterately viewed high schools from the outside in, as an institution whose fundamental purpose is national as well as familial and personal. As Sizer was to do a quarter-century later, he too based his high school reform vision on more than a year of visits to schools throughout the nation, where he and a small group of colleagues talked with students, teachers, and principals. But it was less the incessant dailiness he noticed in these visits than the purpose he constructed for it—a construction influenced, of course, by his nation-building activities in Germany.

A chief function of the high school, as Conant came to articulate it in four books over the course of the next 20 years, is to foster an equality of status and of opportunity among all American youth (Conant, 1959, 1960, 1961, 1967). The high school, he said, brings together in one place at a formative moment in their lives "the future professional man, the future craftsman, the future manager of industry, the future labor leader, the future salesman, and the future engineer" (1967, p. 62). Its purpose is to help each appreciate the value of the other, even as it prepares each for a very different place in the world after high school. This is his framing of the core dilemma.

To manage the dilemma, Conant argued for three radical changes in the high schools of the 1950s. First, they had to get bigger. He deplored the fact that over 70% of American high schools then had 12th grade enrollments of fewer than 100 students (Conant, 1959). Such schools could not in his opinion provide the curricular differentiation necessary to serve equally well both the "academically talented" and the vocationally oriented. Yet he thought it was crucial for democracy to serve both groups within the same institutional context.

Partly because of Conant's advocacy, schools did get bigger. In 1959, he argued for consolidating the 21,000 high schools operating in 1956 into just 9,000. Consolidation never went quite that far in terms of absolute numbers, but in combination with the expansion of the high school population, it accomplished Conant's goal anyway. Today there are roughly 16,000 high schools in the United States, but these enroll at least 60% more students than in 1960 (*Digest of Educational Statistics*, 2000; U.S. Census Bureau, 1960).

Second, Conant argued that high schools had to be more generously and reliably financed. He wanted money drawn from more dependable sources like the federal treasury. On the other hand, he remained conservative in his views concerning school governance. He liked the idea of the local school board, and worried that power might follow money as state and federal governments increased their share of local school financing. It would. However, he thought the need outweighed the risk.

Finally, Conant prescribed a host of changes in the internal organization of the high school, all related to managing the core dilemma. If the list of these changes seems familiar, it is partly because his prescriptions proved so influential. He said high schools should expand guidance services, including aptitude and achievement testing; offer a seven-period day to accommodate an expansion of both required courses and electives (though in his second report, he acknowledged that bloc scheduling and other looser arrangements of time and space might suit as well); abandon "tracks" such as "academic," "commercial," "trade," and so on, but designate most courses by ability level; preserve heterogeneous grouping in homerooms, and also in a 12th-grade course called Problems of Democracy, thus preserving places for social mix; and pay special attention to both "highly gifted pupils" and "very slow readers" (Conant, 1959, 1967).

Today, the widespread practice of designating courses by ability level is also referred to as "tracking." This is because schedulers, scheduling constraints, and students themselves often ensure that individual students' courses are all at the same level. The reasons for this include racism as well as the stereotype threat that racism creates (Steele & Aronson, 1998). Indeed, in making a clear distinction between tracking and ability grouping, Conant was disingenuous at best. The following passage from his book *Slums and Suburbs* (1961) captures both his awareness of the conflation of tracking and ability grouping, and the implicitly racist basis of his denial of its importance: "Such an arrangement [ability grouping in the major subjects] may well isolate Negroes in some schools in the bottom group, but surely there will be considerable mixing in the large middle groups if not in the top group"(p. 64).

Some 20 years after Conant issued his first report, the comprehensive high school, as he imagined and encouraged it, had become the norm in secondary schooling throughout the United States—not only in the small cities whose high schools he had studied, but in most of the metropolitan suburbs, too, and even in most of the big cities (though these also tended to preserve specialty high schools). In the concluding paragraph of his 1960 book, *The Child, the Parent, and the State,* Conant expressed his enormous confidence in the trajectory of reform he had helped launch:

> If the free world survives the perils that now confront it, I believe historians in the year 2059 will regard the American experiment in democracy as a great and successful adventure of the human race. Furthermore, as an essential part of this adventure—indeed, as the basic element in the twentieth century—they will praise the revolutionary transformation of America's treatment of its children and of its youth. They will regard the American high school, as it was perfected by the end of the twentieth century, not only as one of the finest products of democracy, but as a continuing insurance for the preservation of the vitality of a society of free men. (p. 103)

But the core dilemma proved harder to manage than Conant suspected. In fact, the rest of the 20th century would bring several more twists of high school reform—some to loosen, some to tighten up again. And by the end of the century, *perfection* was nowhere in sight.

The loosening reform of the 1970s involved not just the high school's mission and curriculum, as Conant helped shape them, but also its institutional identity. For the first time in 100 years, a significant number of reformers advocated managing the core dilemma by going outside the high school as ordinarily defined. Charles Silberman (1970) captured the spirit of this reform in the introduction to his best-selling *Crisis in the Classroom.* The "crisis" this time, though partly intellectual as in Conant's day, was more substantially moral and aesthetic. Here is how he put it:

> Because adults take the schools so much for granted, they fail to appreciate what grim, joyless places most American schools are, how oppressive and petty are the rules by which they are governed, how intellectually sterile and esthetically barren the atmosphere, what an appalling lack of civility obtains on the part of teachers and principals, what contempt they unconsciously display for children as children. (p. 10)

His critique was the establishment echo (by a respected journalist, funded by the Carnegie Corporation) of more radical critiques of schooling by Edgar Z. Friedenberg (1964, 1965), John Holt (1964), Paul Goodman

(1969), Ivan Illich (1970), A. S. Neill (1960), and others. Its message was abetted by a spate of muckraking books about actual schools, particularly urban ones; and also by books that offered images of alternative kinds of schooling—for example, Joseph Featherstone's (1971) *Schools Where Children Learn,* and at the high school level, John Bremer's and Michael von Moschzisker's (1971) *The School Without Walls.*

Silberman writes that Bremer's Parkway Program in Philadelphia was founded on the premise that the comprehensive high school had by 1970 "reached the end of its development"(Silberman, 1970, quoting Bremer, p. 349). Indeed, throughout the U.S. in these years, a number of *alternative* high schools opened, funded by a federal funding stream focused on the support of innovation, Title III of the Elementary and Secondary Education Act. In New York City, for example, there were dozens of them, some designed from scratch, some incorporating private "street academies" or "free schools" (Phillips, 2000). All defined themselves in opposition to the comprehensive high school: they were smaller, looser, countercultural. As Bremer suggested, they were not about reforming the high school, but about moving beyond it. Some, like Bremer's school, proved short-lived— victims of the systems they tried to subvert. Others, however, survived much longer. The New York City alternative schools, for example, grew to some 70 schools in 2003 before the name *alternative* was dropped. To- day the schools remain influential in the city and beyond, many of them helping to spearhead what has been called the "small schools movement" (Toch, 2003).

Meanwhile, another reform began to gather energy in the early 1980s. Initially aimed at saving the comprehensive high school, it led directly to two different strains of reform. The first wittingly undermines the compre- hensive high school, while the second unwittingly does so. This tightening reform got national momentum quickly with the release of the report by the National Commission on Excellence in Education in 1983. Entitled *A Nation at Risk,* the report focused especially on the high school. "The public has no patience," it said, "with undemanding and superfluous high school offerings"(p. 17). The nation's educational mediocrity would have seemed an act of war, it declared further, if the mediocrity had been im- posed by a foreign power. "We have . . . squandered . . . gains in student achievement, . . . dismantled essential support systems. . . . We have, in ef- fect, been committing an act of unthinking, unilateral educational disar- mament" (p. 5).

A Nation at Risk attacked the practices of the comprehensive high school, but by no means the idea of it.

We must emphasize, that the variety of student aspirations, abilities, and prep- aration requires that appropriate content be available to satisfy diverse needs.

> . . . We must demand the best effort and performance from all students,
> whether they are gifted or less able, affluent or disadvantaged, whether des-
> tined for college, the farm, or industry. (p. 24)

This is the rhetoric of the comprehensive high school. The problem, it im-
plied, was that the practices of most high schools failed to honor this rhetoric. The solution, it said, was to shape up: every high school student should
be required to study harder, learn more, spend more time in school.

The report's bellicose rhetoric seemed to seize the imagination of the
general public, and the Department of Education responded to requests for
six million copies (Chubb & Moe, 1990). However, it alienated reformers
on the left whose support for alternative schools and other loosening efforts had roots in the anti–Vietnam War movement. Moreover, the harsh-
ness of its critique encouraged a group of reformers on the right to doubt
whether the high school—and, indeed, public schooling in general—could
or ought to be saved. Milton Friedman, the conservative economist, had
proposed as early as 1955 that the United States replace what he viewed as
a monopolistic system of government-run public schooling with a market-
oriented one. The mechanism for such a transformation, he argued, was
the educational voucher, issued to families and redeemable at a school of
their choice. It drew little attention at first, but gained currency later among
conservative critics of schooling (Moe, 2001). John Chubb and Terry
Moe's 1990 book, *Politics, Markets, and America's Schools,* proved particularly influential in this regard.

By the end of the 1990s, the idea of market-based school reform had
begun to gain broader political appeal. It helped that in the late 1980s and
early 1990s school choice began to become associated with equity-minded
policymaking rather than its opposite, the "freedom of choice" plans that
some Southern communities had earlier used to preserve segregation. One
mechanism this time was the magnet school. The efforts by cities and metropolitan areas to desegregate their schools without relying on mandatory
school assignment by race suddenly encouraged differentiation across
schools, including high schools, by mission and curriculum. Then in 1990
the Wisconsin legislature approved the first public voucher plan, to provide
options for Milwaukee's poorest families (Moe, 2001); and in 1991, working on the supply side of the schooling market, Minnesota introduced the
nation's first charter schools (Finn, Vanourek, & Manno, 2000; Nathan,
1996).

However, the influence of *A Nation at Risk* was hardly confined to
the encouragement of market-based schooling. It is customary also to trace
the start of standards-based school reform to the report. In contrast to the
market reformers, however, standards reformers are tighteners. In the case
of the high school, they advocate a high-level common curriculum for all

students. *A Nation at Risk* did not propose that all high school students study the same things at the same level: three years of mathematics for all, yes, but not necessarily the same mathematics. But the report's emphasis on rigor and on the use of criterion-based rather than aptitude-based testing nonetheless makes it a legitimate progenitor of the standards movement.

Standards-based reformers aim to manage the high school's core dilemma by effectively denying it. Because of changes in the economy, they argue, public purpose and private interest should be reconciled; society demands that all students now be educated to high levels of distinction (Marshall & Tucker, 1992). If states give the same academically rigorous, high-stakes exit exams to everyone, they say, teachers and students will rise to the challenge.

James Conant would have been astonished by their argument. In his 1960 book, *The Child, the Parent, and the State,* he ridicules a 1958 proposal to the Georgia legislature to mandate that all high school students in that state study four years of mathematics and science. As he put it later, "There are a large number of youths who are either unwilling or unable to do the amount of work" implicit in such mandates; to force them would risk their health (1967, p. 47).

A DIFFERENT ANGLE

When *A Nation at Risk* was released, Theodore Sizer, having recently left Andover, was busy preparing his own report on the high school, published the next year as *Horace's Compromise*. It was one of three reports from A Study of High Schools, which Sizer and his colleagues began in 1979 (Hampel, 1986; Powell et al.; 1985; and Sizer, 1984). The study was sponsored by the National Association of Secondary School Principals and the National Association of Independent Schools. The Carnegie Corporation, which had previously funded both Conant's and Silberman's studies, helped fund this one, too. The study combined relatively brief visits to a wide variety of high schools with more intensive investigations of a particular sample of them, and it also included historical inquiry.

A Study of High Schools had three major findings. The first concerned curriculum: whether in urban public, suburban public, or private settings, the researchers found the curriculum of the high school both shallow and disconnected. Students did not acquire depth of understanding in any subject, and what they learned about one subject seldom connected with any other. The second finding concerned teachers: they were dysfunctionally isolated and also dysfunctionally harried. And the third finding concerned students: they were mostly passive, and they were mostly anonymous. The culture of instruction in the high school defined students as listeners, note-takers, answer-makers. And the structures of the place practically ensured that no student was known in any integrated way by any single adult. Years after the study, Sizer (1999) provided an image of the latter for an article in the *American School Board Journal:*

> My name is Michael. I am 16, an 11th grader at Regional High. My little sister goes there too. So do 1,500 other kids. It's a friendly place. A typical day starts with homeroom. About 20 of us are checked in by Ms. Blake. We pledge alle-giance to the flag, hear announcements over the PA, and chat. Ms. Blake usually spends the time collecting her papers and books. . . . Last week I had my first scheduled appointment with my counselor about college plans. He asked a lot of questions and put my answers on a form. I forget his name. (p. 29)

By contrast, here is Conant (1959) viewing one piece of the same terri-tory, but from a very different angle of vision:

> The main concern of the counselor in a suburban high school is often with the overambitious parent who wants his offspring to go to a particular college, even if the pupil has less-than-average academic ability. . . . The answer to this . . . situation is policy—defensible policy. For instance, the guidance de-partment must have it as policy that parents who want their children prepared for colleges for which they are obviously unsuited will be resisted. (p. 93)

There are major similarities as well as important differences between these two reformers' ideas, but above all there is the important difference of perspective. Although both attend to the high school's core dilemma, involving the tug between public purpose and private interest, one inveter-ately views the dilemma first from the public side, while the other views it first from the personal side—the perspective of a student like Michael or of a teacher like Horace.

Shortly after publishing *Horace's Compromise,* Sizer founded the Co-alition of Essential Schools (CES). His next two books, *Horace's School* (1992) and *Horace's Hope* (1996), drew on his experience chairing this national network of schools active in reform. Indeed, Sizer's continuing involvement with CES has, in effect, stretched A Study of High Schools to date into a 20-year project. The CES Network promotes 10 principles of reform. Two of these, in juxtaposition, capture succinctly the core dilemma of the high school. The first is that the high school should have universal goals for all students; and the second is that it should respect the fact that students differ.

As Conant shaped it, the comprehensive high school seeks to honor the first of these principles by being an institution open to all the teenagers of the community—a big public facility through which everyone passes and within which everyone interacts. In the process, they all get socialized in particular ways. At the same time, it honors the second principle by providing varied social and academic offerings, from which students make individual selections. Some go to the prom, some don't; some take calculus, some never get past algebra. In this way, the high school may be said to have a deliberately fuzzy intellectual mission, but a clear cultural one. The high school is the place, as the authors of *The Shopping Mall High School* put it, where nearly all Americans "park while working out the social problems of becoming adults" (Powell et al., 1985, p. 237).

As Sizer would have us manage the dilemma, by contrast, the high school has a clear intellectual and cultural mission, but it turns fuzzy on the details. That is because for him the details are properly a matter of intimacy rather than of generality. For Conant's outside-in, policy-focused perspective, Sizer substitutes an inside-out, familial one. As he sees it, "The heart of schooling is found in relationships between student, teacher, and ideas. Kids differ, and serious ideas affect each one in often interestingly different ways, especially as that child matures" (Sizer, 1996, p. xiii). Yet serious ideas, he says, are for every student. Indeed, for him, the fundamental purpose of high school is intellectual (another of the CES principles). One manages the dilemma of teaching all students how to use their minds well by knowing them well and then by tailoring an intellectually demanding education to suit each one of them. This is a matter of attitude, he suggests, not of policy and structure.

In the process of making this argument, Sizer cuts through the rhetoric on both sides of the tracking debate, a debate conceived in reaction to Conant's design—whether the high school should have heterogeneously grouped classes or homogeneously grouped ones (Oakes, 1985). Remember that Conant argued for mostly homogeneous ones, but for heterogeneous homerooms and courses on problems in democracy. Sizer argues instead that the unit of interest ought to be the individual student, not the classroom. In *The Students Are Watching* (1999), a book co-authored with his wife, Nancy Faust Sizer, a veteran high school teacher, the Sizers propose that each high school student have his or her own unique "track." "Sorting is a fact of life," they explain, "and not necessarily a bad one. A sorting system which is flexible and reasonably respectful of people's wishes is essential. The trick is always to make the deliberate sorting as thoughtful as possible, harming as few people as possible" (p. 79).

But can the comprehensive high school be redesigned along these lines—to sort without stigma? At first Sizer thought so. Indeed, his 1992 book, *Horace's School,* offered a blueprint for such a design. Today, however, he says he would write a different book if he had it to do over (Sizer, personal communication, 2002). Some traditional high schools that he knows have managed to make the transition, but with great difficulty, and their achievements remain precarious, subject to shifts in leadership and policy. For this reason, he now advocates more radical reform. He is especially enthusiastic about charter schools, having founded one (the Parker School) himself with neighbors in his hometown, and having (with Nancy Sizer) spent a year as the school's co-acting principal.

But long before the existence of the Parker School, there were hints of Sizer's dissatisfaction with the very institution of the high school (as conventionally defined) in his 1973 book on school reform, *Places for Learning, Places for Joy*. Here he raises what might be called constitutional questions. Should American schools really be both government-funded *and* government-managed? It was not always so, he says. Nor is it so at the level of tertiary American education. "Harvard [where he was then Dean] may be privately managed," he explains, "but it is very much a public university in the sense that it spends government money and allocates this in ways mandated by public authorities" (p. 19). Should schooling be compulsory, particularly if it means having no choice but to attend one particular school? Should it be locally controlled—that is, by local political authorities? Should it be utterly secular—particularly if this means avoiding moral education? Does it have to be academic in order to be intellectually focused? That is, does it have to follow either the university's disciplines or Eliot's "subjects" in order to teach students to use their minds well?

These questions arose from Sizer's historical perspective on secondary schools, not just the high schools but the academies; from his avowed sympathy with some of the 1970s curriculum reformers—for example, Jerome Bruner and his *Man, A Course of Study*—who were then busily violating the borders among Eliot's main-line subjects (Dow, 1991); and perhaps also from a latent sympathy with some of the 1970s most radical school critics—for example, John Holt (1972), whose criticism eventually turned to advocacy for homeschooling and other alternatives. The questions that Sizer raised in 1971 are loosening questions of a certain kind—not aimed, for example, at making the high school curriculum more elective, as less radical critics at the time were suggesting, but rather at provoking some wonder about how we define school, including *high* school. They forecast his linkage with this era's looseners—the market-based reformers, and the small-school reformers.

It is not surprising that Sizer today is a major critic of standards-based reform. His critique is different, however, from the one that Conant might have offered, though similarly steeped in a concern for how to manage the high school's core dilemma. Given the economy of the mid-20th century, it was possible to imagine—as Conant clearly did—that a high school's

graduates could be both socially equal and also unevenly prepared intellectually. But by the late 1980s, as both Sizer and the standards-based reformers recognized, this way of managing the dilemma seemed no longer viable.
Yes, there are today and will continue to be American jobs that are not
"knowledge-based," but for the most part, these jobs do not pay enough
to keep a family out of poverty—and one cannot be "socially equal" when
in poverty (Murnane & Levy, 1996). The response of the standards-based
reformers to this economic reality has been to try to abolish curricular
differentiation. Sizer's response, by contrast, has been to argue instead that
we need to diversify our sense of what it means to use one's mind well, and
also our sense of what it means to be *high*ly schooled. The first involves, as
his longtime friend and colleague Deborah Meier (1995) puts it, abandon-
ing our old habit of confusing the intellectual with the academic; while
the second means encouraging not just new high school designs, but new
conceptions of secondary education.

BACK TO THE FUTURE

School reform in the United States today is dominated by standards-based
reform, with its logic of test-driven change, standardized curriculum, and
high outcomes for all. Standards-based reform is the product of a remark-
able political alliance that coalesced in the mid-1980s, and has gone on to
affect educational policymaking deeply at federal, state, and local levels.
Its members include economic leaders who have come to regard an intellectually able workforce as an important form of capital (Gerstner, 1994);
politicians at virtually all levels of the political system who see in the formulations of standards-based reform an intuitively obvious solution to the
economic dislocation that so many American families and communities began experiencing in the 1980s; and civil rights leaders who hope that standards-based reform may be an avenue toward equity at last (Price, 2002).

Standards-based reform aims to undo the most deeply embedded features of the comprehensive high school, namely variable curriculum and
variable expectations. Yet, remarkably, most standards-based policies take
for granted the continuation of the comprehensive high school. It is as if
the design Conant championed could stay otherwise intact even as it lost
its ideological foundation.

This seems unlikely. Although standards-based reform aims to tighten
the high school's mission and curriculum, its ultimate impact may be to
loosen the high school's grip on secondary education. In effect, it may
tighten a turn too far. This is especially likely if high-stakes testing leads
to a dramatic reversal of 100 years of inclining high school graduation

rates. Indeed, there is irony in the very fact that a reform focused on high standards for all would rely so heavily on standardized testing. Early 20th-century reformers adopted what was then the new technology of standardized testing specifically for its power to *differentiate* finely among students. They would hardly have understood how or why it might be used some 80 years later to encourage students to become more alike. Moreover, some contemporary testing experts argue that the technologies of standardized testing are inherently unsuitable to such a task (Heubert & Hauser, 1998; Orfield & Kornhaber, 2001).

Ultimately, the prevalence of the high school as we have come to know it depends on the perception that it can manage the core dilemma—serve both a significant public purpose, and also satisfy the individual interests of youth. If increasing numbers of students are pushed out of high schools either by administrators who want to keep their accountability scores high or by the students' own perceptions that the institution is not for them, then we are likely to see conditions that hasten the diversification of secondary schooling. There are signs of this in the big cities, where many high schools are manifestly failing to meet individual interests, and where pressures are growing to introduce vouchers and charters, and to create small schools on either a stand-alone basis or by breaking up big schools into small schools-within-schools. There is some research indicating that youth are better served in small schools, particularly urban youth (Cotton, 1996; Wasley et al., 2000). And the small-school strategy to improve the high school was recently given a psychological and financial boost by the Bill and Melinda Gates Foundation, as well as some other funders, including the Carnegie Corporation (rounding off a century of reform efforts).

Meanwhile, there are also threats to the comprehensive high school from the other side of the core dilemma. These arise from a perception that it no longer serves an important public purpose, which just happens to be the one that originally propelled it to dominance, namely the direct preparation of students for jobs in the American economy. This is the message of reformers associated with the school-to-work movement. Adria Steinberg (1998), for example, makes a persuasive case that the comprehensive high school is too big, too inflexible in its structures, and too removed from the real world to provide youth the kind of education that will enable them to thrive in an economy that prizes resourcefulness over dutifulness, and readiness to learn over ready-made skills. She advocates small schools prepared to help their students exploit the intellectual potential of internships and projects in nearby economies. For example, both she and Elliot Levine (2002) point to a public institution for secondary education in Providence, Rhode Island, that does not even have the words *high school* in its name. The Metropolitan Regional Career and Technical Center (MET), founded by entrepreneurial educators Dennis Littky and Elliot Washor (longtime associates of Theodore Sizer), is not part of a school district, offers no classes, and confines its enrollment to 100 high-school-age students per each of its several campuses. The students follow their own individualized curriculum, negotiated with an advisor, one that mixes individual and group projects, apprenticeships in the local economy, and Internet-based learning.

Will the rest of this century bring many METs, plus a hundred varieties of other secondary schools? It is, of course, much too early to tell whether the century's predominant pattern of secondary schooling will more resemble that of the last century, or of the one before. What seems clear, however, is that Conant's prediction concerning the long-lived universality of the comprehensive high school is unlikely to prove true. Where particular communities perceive that the comprehensive high school still manages well the core dilemma between public purpose and private interest, it is likely to survive. But where perceptions run the other way, its clients may well give it up.

REFERENCES

Bremer, J., & von Moschzisker, M. (1971). *The school without walls: Philadelphia's parkway program.* New York: Holt, Rinehart, and Winston.

Chubb, J. E., & Moe, T. M. (1990). *Politics, markets, and America's schools.* Washington, D.C.: The Brookings Institution.

Cohen, D. K., & Neufeld, B. (1981). The failure of high schools and the progress of education. *Daedulus, 110,* 69–89.

Conant, J. B. (1959). *The American high school today: A first report to interested citizens.* New York: McGraw-Hill.

Conant, J. B. (1960). *The child, the parent, and the state.* Cambridge, MA: Harvard University Press.

Conant, J. B. (1961). *Slums and suburbs: A commentary on schools in metropolitan areas.* New York: McGraw-Hill.

Conant, J. B. (1967). *The comprehensive high school: A second report to interested citizens.* New York: McGraw-Hill.

Cotton, K. (1996). *School size, school climate, and student performance* (School Improvement Research Series, Close-Up #20). Portland, OR: Northwest Regional Educational Laboratory.

Digest of Educational Statistics. (2000). Chapter 2, elementary and secondary education, Table 99. Washington, D.C.: National Center for Educational Statistics.

Dow, P. B. (1991). *Schoolhouse politics: Lessons from the Sputnik era.* Cambridge, MA: Harvard University Press.

Featherstone, J. (1971). *Schools where children learn.* New York: Liveright.

Finn, C. E., Vanourek, G., & Manno, B. V. (2000). *Charter schools in action: Renewing public education.* Princeton, NJ: Princeton University Press.

Friedenberg, E. Z. (1964). *Coming of age in America.* New York: Random House.

Friedenberg, E. Z. (1965). *The dignity of youth and other atavisms.* Boston: Beacon Press.

Friedman, M. (1955). The role of government in education. In R. A. Solo (Ed.), *Economics and the public interest* (pp. 123–144). New Brunswick, NJ: Rutgers University Press.

Gerstner, L. V. (1994). *Reinventing education: Entrepreneurship in today's schools.* New York: Dutton.

Gleason, P. (1995). *Contending with modernity: Catholic higher education in twentieth-century America.* New York: Oxford University Press.

Goodman, P. (1969). *Compulsory mis-education.* New York: Horizon Press.

Hampel, R. L. (1986). *The last little citadel.* Boston: Houghton Mifflin.

Heubert, J. P., & Hauser, R. M. (Eds.). (1998). *High stakes: Testing for tracking, promotion, and graduation.* Washington, D.C.: National Academy Press.

Holt, J. (1964). *How children fail.* New York: Pitman Publishing.

Holt, J. (1972). *Freedom and beyond.* New York: E. P. Dutton.

Illich, I. (1970). *De-schooling society.* New York: Harper & Row.

Krug, E. A. (1964). *The shaping of the American high school.* New York: Harper & Row.

Krug, E. A. (1972). *The shaping of the American high school. Vol. 2: 1920–1941.* Madison: University of Wisconsin Press.

Labaree, D. F. (1988). *The making of an American high school: The credentials market and the Central High School of Philadelphia, 1838–1939.* New Haven: Yale University Press.

Levine, E. (2002). *One kid at a time: Big lessons from a small school.* New York: Teachers College Press.

Marshall, R., & Tucker, M. (1992). *Thinking for a living: Education and the wealth of nations.* New York: Basic.

Meier, D. (1995). *Power of their ideas: Lessons for America from a small school in Harlem.* Boston: Beacon Press.

Moe, T. M. (2001). *Schools, vouchers, and the American public.* Washington, D.C.: Brookings Institution Press.

Murnane, R. J., & Levy, F. (1996). *Teaching the new basic skills: Principles for educating children to thrive in a changing economy.* New York: The Free Press.

Nathan, J. (1996). *Charter schools: Creating hope and opportunity for American education.* San Franciso: Jossey Bass.

National Commission on Excellence in Education. (1983). *A nation at risk.* Washington, D.C.: U. S. Government Printing Office.

Neill, A. S. (1960). *Summerhill.* New York: Hart.

Oakes, J. (1985). *Keeping track: How schools structure inequality.* New Haven: Yale University Press.

Orfield, G., & Kornhaber, M. (Eds.). (2001). *Raising standards or raising barriers?*

Inequality and high stakes testing in public education. New York: Century Foundation Press.

Phillips, S. (2000). *Alternative schools in New York City.* Presentation to the Seminar on the Future of the Comprehensive High School, New York University.

Powell, A., Farrar, E., & Cohen, D. K. (1985). *The shopping-mall high school: Winners and losers in the education marketplace.* Boston: Houghton Mifflin.

Price, H. B. (2002). *Achievement matters: Getting your child the best education possible.* New York: Kensington.

Reese, W. J. (1995). *The origins of the American high school.* New Haven: Yale University Press.

Silberman, C. E. (1970). *Crisis in the classroom: The remaking of American education.* New York: Random House.

Sizer, T. R. (Ed). (1964a). *The age of the academies.* New York: Bureau of Publications, Teachers College, Columbia University.

Sizer, T. R. (1964b). *Secondary schools at the turn of the century.* New Haven: Yale University Press.

Sizer, T. R. (1973). *Places for learning, places for joy: Speculations on American school reform.* Cambridge, MA: Harvard University Press.

Sizer, T. R. (1984). *Horace's compromise: The dilemma of the American high school.* Boston: Houghton Mifflin.

Sizer, T. R. (1986). Foreward to R. L. Hampel, *The last little citadel.* Boston: Houghton Mifflin.

Sizer, T. R. (1992). *Horace's school: Redesigning the American high school.* Boston: Houghton Mifflin.

Sizer, T. R. (1996). *Horace's hope: What works for the American high school.* Boston: Houghton Mifflin.

Sizer, T. R. (1999). Michael alone. *American School Board Journal.* September, 29.

Sizer, T. R., & Sizer, N. F. (1999). *The students are watching.* Boston: Beacon.

Steele, C., & Aronson, J. (1998). Stereotype threat and the test performance of academically successful African-Americans. In Christopher Jencks & Meredith Phillips (Eds.), *The black-white test score gap* (pp. 401–427). Washington, D.C.: The Brookings Institution.

Steinberg, A. (1998). *Real learning, real work: School-to-work as high school reform.* New York: Routledge.

Toch, T. (2003). *High schools on a human scale.* Boston: Beacon.

U.S. Bureau of Education. (1918). *Cardinal principles of secondary education.* Bulletin 1918, number 35, Department of the Interior. Washington, D.C.: U.S. Government Printing Office.

U. S. Census Bureau. (1960). *School enrollment and educational attainment for the United States: 1960.* PC(S1)-20. Washington, D.C.: U.S. Department of Commerce.

Wasley, P., Fine, M., Gladden, M., Holland, N. E., King, S. P., Mosak, E., & Powell, L. C. (2000). *Small schools, great strides: A study of new small schools in Chicago.* New York: Bank Street College of Education.

3

The Problems of Educating Urban Youth

James B. Conant and the Changing Context of Metropolitan America, 1945–1995

JOHN L. RURY

In a sense, this book both honors and questions he work of James Bryant Conant, who issued his famous report, *The American High School Today*, in 1959, giving voice to a clear and influential reaffirmation of the comprehensive secondary school. Just two years later he published *Slums and Suburbs* (1961), comparing schools in poor and affluent communities. The first of these books was about the nation as a whole; the second focused on the country's major metropolitan areas. Conant's vision in these two works makes an interesting point of departure for consideration of the forces that have shaped the American high school in the latter half of the 20th century. The question is whether the comprehensive high school is possible—or even considered desirable—in a society as divided by race, social class, and culture as the United States is today. It is especially germane in metropolitan America, where about 80% of American youth live and learn at the end of the 20th century (Fox, 1985; Goldsmith & Blakely, 1992).

As suggested in other chapters in this volume, the comprehensive high school, as defined by the *Cardinal Principles* report of 1918 (Commission on the Reorganization of Secondary Education, 1918), was premised on the idea of the common school (Hampel, 1986; Krug, 1972). This was a point that especially impressed Conant, perhaps because of his own plebian origins. Even as students were differentiated into various courses of study, they were supposed to be bound together in a common academic core, and in the social and cultural life of the high school as an institution (Conant, 1959). During the 20th century the comprehensive high school became a model for school districts across the country, including those in large cities (Cremin, 1961; Herbst, 1996). This was a break with the past, when specialization had prevailed, particularly in urban secondary schools. In this respect the somewhat narrow vocationalism characteristic of an earlier era was replaced by the democratic ethos of the comprehensive high school (Krug, 1972).

Conant wrote about secondary education during a time of profound changes in American life, and in the nation's secondary schools. This was especially true in major metropolitan areas, and it is in this context that the implications of Conant's work can be best understood. Several major trends in the postwar period affected the American high school, making Conant's vision problematic. The first of these was the changing racial and ethnic composition of the nation's principal metropolitan areas. With the migration of millions of poorly educated African Americans to the North during the late 1940s, 1950s and 1960s, public schools systems became differentiated along racial lines. Growing inequalities in the type and quality of education came to characterize metropolitan life (Kantor & Brenzel, 1993). A second major development was the appearance of a vibrant, pervasive, and commercially expansive youth culture in the postwar period. This was partly a consequence of numbers, particularly the large "baby boom" cohort of the 1950s and 1960s (Hawes & Hiner, 1985). With growing high school attendance, followed by rising college enrollments, educational institutions became the location in which these emerging forms of adolescent culture could develop most rapidly (Coleman, 1961). Finally, there was the evolution of the American economy in the postwar period, particularly the changing sectoral distribution of the occupational structure, and rising educational requirements for different types of jobs. The result was that the vocational educational options that Conant and other proponents of the comprehensive high school believed would serve a majority of American high school students were increasingly irrelevant to the demands of the job market.

These developments affected the ability of secondary schools to realize the ideals that Conant and other proponents of the comprehensive high school had identified for them. The publication of *Slums and Suburbs* demonstrated Conant's awareness of these challenges, at least in part. This book examined the problem of racial segregation in education, and the many dimensions of social and economic inequality that accompanied it. It also considered the relationship of high schools to the economy, and the growing preoccupation of affluent families with college admissions. Conant (1961) acknowledged that in larger cities and their suburban communities, truly comprehensive high schools would be difficult to realize. In fact, he estimated that only about 40% of American high schools fit the comprehensive model at the end of the 1950s (Conant, 1959). Yet he remained hopeful that the spirit of a common secondary school could be realized in spite of such limitations.

In the discussion that follows, each of the major challenges to Conant's vision is explored in greater depth, along with their implications for American high schools in the postwar period. While Conant helped to articulate a democratic conception of secondary education and its purposes in a capitalistic society, it seems that history has made that goal an elusive one. This poses a formidable task for educators interested in achieving it for the future.

RACE AND THE COMPREHENSIVE HIGH SCHOOL

Conant's 1959 report, which reaffirmed the ideal of the comprehensive high school, did not address the question of race. And in the years following publication of the Conant report, race became the overriding issue in the nation's principal urban school districts. Race came to affect the spatial organization of cities in ways that other facets of social organization had not. Blacks were highly segregated from whites, a feature of urban life that was enforced with violence, as well as with legal and quasi-legal action (Massey & Denton, 1993). Educational resources, of course, were also spatially distributed, a point Conant recognized in writing *Slums and Suburbs*. This, as he acknowledged, posed perhaps the greatest challenge to the comprehensive high school as a basic institution of American civilization.

Much of this, of course, is well known. World War II had barely ended when a grand migration to suburbia began in most of the nation's largest cities. Pressured by severe housing shortages in the central cities, and encouraged by public policies that stimulated road-building and guaranteed cheap private transportation, Americans began flocking to newly opened developments on the fringes of the urban core areas. Between 1940 and 1960, the country's suburban population grew by some 27 million, or more than twice the numerical increase in the population of central cities during the same period. As a result, the share of the metropolitan area population living in central cities dropped from nearly 63% in 1940 to 59% in 1950, and to 51% in 1960. The decline continued thereafter, and by 1980 only

40% of the country's metropolitan area population lived in central cities, with the rest in surrounding suburbs (Fox, 1985; Jackson, 1985; Teaford, 1990).

Migrants from central cities were disproportionately young, middle class, and upwardly mobile. The availability of Veterans Administration (VA) and Federal Housing Authority (FHA) loans in the decades immediately following World War II, along with housing shortages in central cities, made the suburbs especially attractive to new families. The expanding economy provided a stable source of employment, particularly in downtown office complexes but also in rapidly developing suburban retail and manufacturing centers. These families could afford to buy housing in the suburbs, and held jobs that allowed them to spend the time and incur the costs involved in daily commuting. A post-war "marriage boom" added more than ten million new households within a decade. And the baby boom made relatively cheap homes in suburban subdivisions difficult to resist (Fox, 1985; Palen, 1992).

Suburban migrants were also overwhelmingly white. By 1960, when the suburban population exceeded that of the central cities, less than 5% of suburbanites were African American (Goldsmith & Blakely, 1992). Thirty years later they were less than 10%, and were largely segregated in separate suburban communities. This was partly because of subtle but effective practices of exclusion that discouraged African Americans from buying homes in suburban areas. As a group, whites were allowed to move into these new, burgeoning, affluent communities on the edge of the expanding metropolitan area. And as they moved to suburbia, the populations of the country's central cities became older, poorer, and darker (Jackson, 1985; Massey & Denton, 1993; Teaford, 1990).

The proportion of the central city population that is white has diminished each decade since 1950, falling from more than 80% to about a third in the 1990s. While the African-American population increased rapidly in the 1950s and 1960s, leveling off at about a third of central city residents, the number of Hispanics has increased significantly since the 1970s. As William Julius Wilson (1987) has noted, poverty levels have increased significantly among all groups of city residents in the closing decades of the 20th century, but particularly among African-Americans. Whereas some 11% of central-city residents were poor in the mid-1970s, and 18% of central-city African-Americans, by 1990 the figures had jumped to almost 20% and 34%, respectively (Goldsmith & Blakely, 1992).

It was the early stages of this process of change that Conant confronted at the end of the 1950s. The decades following World War II witnessed a profound transformation of American metropolitan areas, creating a new cultural geography defined by race and income. This had a dramatic effect on many aspects of life in the nation's major metropolitan areas. It meant that for large numbers of urban and suburban residents there were few shared public spaces and social experiences. Stereotypical images fostered by the development of mass media created an atmosphere of mistrust and fear (Fox, 1985). And one area where this process had an almost immediate impact was public education. The disparity between city and suburban schools was a major theme in *Slums and Suburbs,* and Conant (1961) described going from one institution to another as "a profoundly shocking experience" (p. 80).

Beginning in the 1950s, questions of equity in black and white schooling became critical policy issues facing urban school districts (Rury, 1999). In the nation's urban high schools, the question of race came to be a source of great dissention, a point of differentiation that defined the institution in new ways. The 1954 *Brown* decision helped to put schools at the very center of the emerging national civil rights movement. In large metropolitan areas this led to conflict over desegregation and equality, initially in the South but eventually in other regions also (Hochschild, 1985). In the major urban areas the impact of these issues was decisive. The NAACP and other civil rights organizations pressed school districts aggressively on questions of equity and fairness in education. Old policies of permitting African-American schools to remain overcrowded and understaffed were challenged, even though changes were slow to be realized. Significantly, Conant wrote *Slums and Suburbs* before the question of inequities between black and white schools had become a volatile political issue, and before urban school districts were beset with vehement demonstrations of African-American dissatisfaction (Mirel, 1993, Rury, 1999).

In the years to follow these conflicts escalated as the African-American population of urban school districts approached a majority, particularly in large Northern cities. Despite challenges to racial exclusion, schools remained highly segregated, closely mirroring patterns of residential segregation in urban areas (Orfield et al., 1996; Rury, 1999). This was clearly evident in secondary education. A 1964 study of the Chicago public schools, conducted in the wake of protests over unequal education, demonstrated such tendencies in stark terms (Havighurst, 1964). In all but four schools, the student body was nearly 90% or more African American or white, despite the fact that the district's population was almost evenly divided between these groups. The vast majority of predominantly black schools, moreover, reported low achievement scores and high dropout rates. This pattern was evident in other large cities in this period (Harrison, 1972). The movement of African Americans into Northern urban school districts was marked by high levels of segregation—or racial isolation—and telling black–white differences in educational outcomes (Mirel, 1993;

Stolee, 1993; Wells & Crain, 1997). It was a situation that did not bode well for Conant's vision of the comprehensive high school.

Conant's recognition of the underlying causes of these problems, of course, led him to write *Slums and Suburbs,* but his vision was limited, and many of his recommendations seem naïve in retrospect. He was hardly a proponent of desegregation, and when he visited Chicago to collect data for the *American High School Today* he did not publish school-level statistics, to avoid fanning controversy over the question of racial inequities (Hampel, 1986). The differences Conant observed in writing *Slums and Suburbs* led him to acknowledge the limits of comprehensive schools as a model for big-city school districts. A strong proponent of neighborhood schools, he was willing to accept segregation but hoped for improvements in city schools:

> Antithetical to our free society as I believe *de jure* segregation to be, I think it would be far better for those who are agitating for the deliberate mixing of children to accept *de facto* segregated schools as a consequence of the present housing situation and to work for the improvement of slums schools whether Negro or white. (p. 31)

Unfortunately, there were no easy answers to the dilemma posed by the disparities in educational and social resources on either side of the educational divide. A proponent of ability grouping, Conant appeared to be willing to accept the fact of African-American students being overrepresented in the lowest achievement tracks, or relegated to vocational programs. "Such an arrangement," he wrote, "may well isolate Negroes in some schools in the bottom group, but surely there will be considerable mixing in the large middle groups if not in the top group" (p. 84). These questions, of course, became the focal point of great conflict in the 1960s and beyond, and continue to be matters of controversy today.

Conant also underestimated rates of change in the severity of the problems he identified. Degrees of segregation and differences in achievement would grow even starker in the years to come, as ever-larger numbers of middle-class whites left urban school districts (Kozol, 1991; Wells & Crain, 1997). In Chicago, which he cited as a model of responsible governance in public education, non-Hispanic whites comprised less than 20% of the student body by 1980, and in 1990 they were barely a tenth. This made meaningful integration, particularly in the system's 60 large high schools, a virtual impossibility (Chicago Assembly, 1998; Kleppner, 1984). The ideal of the high school functioning as a microcosm of American society was inconceivable in these circumstances.

The story elsewhere was similar, despite a growing movement to affect desegregation in urban school systems. In 1972 the *Keyes* decision in Denver opened the door to federally mandated desegregation in Northern and Western districts, ruling that public school authorities could be held liable for segregation despite residential patterns. By then, however, the term "white flight" had become a part of the national vocabulary, as large numbers of middle-class whites left city school districts for the suburbs. The *Millikan I* decision in Detroit just two years later foreclosed the possibility of legally mandated desegregation plans across urban-suburban district lines. In this case the Supreme Court ruled that suburban districts could not be compelled to participate in court-ordered busing plans with urban schools. This meant that white families opposed to desegregation could simply leave the city to avoid integrated schools. As a result, the racial profile of schools on either side of the big-city district lines became quite stark. By the 1980s a shrinking minority of urban public school students were white, and an even smaller—though growing—portion of suburban students were African American (Orfield et al., 1996). In the meantime, the portion of the nation's population living outside metropolitan areas continued to decline (Goldsmith & Blakely, 1992). If Conant had hoped that schools in nonmetropolitan communities would provide the model for others to follow, this became less tenable with time.

These changes had a particularly big impact on the culture of American high schools. As secondary education in major metropolitan areas became characterized by a sharp pattern of racial segregation, it was closely associated in the public mind with perceptions about the quality of education (Wells & Crain, 1997). This was evident in the early 1960s in large Northern cities, and became ever more pronounced as the desegregation struggles in public education reached a peak in the 1970s (Hochschild, 1985; Orfield, 1978). High schools became points of conflict when neighborhoods shifted from white to black, and they functioned as bellweathers of academic distinction as graduation rates were publicized and students competed for college admission. Of course, Conant had examined these issues in *Slums and Suburbs,* but the differences between urban and suburban high schools grew even more striking in the decades that followed. By the end of the 1980s there were relatively few public high schools in large cities with a significant number of white students, and few such schools that could be classified as academically excellent (Bettis, 1996; Mora, 1997; Sexton & Nickel, 1992). In short, urban and suburban school districts became ever more disparate in the years following the protracted struggle over desegregation (Stone, 1998).

In the four decades since Conant wrote *The American High School Today,* the common school experience in secondary education appears to have become increasingly elusive. While *Slums and Suburbs* was remarkably prescient in certain ways, Conant clearly underestimated the magnitude of the problems he identified. Residential segregation, which has changed little with the growth of large minority populations in American cities, has led to reduced heterogeneity in many high schools' student bodies, at least outside of the South (Orfield et al., 1996; Rumberger & Willms, 1992). As metropolitan areas have grown in size and complexity, and political conflict has embraced the schools, these patterns of differentiation have deepened their salience. If the comprehensive high school was supposed to bring students from different backgrounds together, it certainly has not succeeded in accomplishing this in the nation's major metropolitan areas, at least as concerns the questions of race and social class (Mora, 1997; Wells & Crain, 1997). In this respect, and in these settings, Conant's vision for the nation certainly has not been fulfilled.

THE RISE OF A YOUTH CULTURE

In *The American High School Today* Conant was concerned about school size, but the high schools in American cities had been large and socially diverse for a long time (Angus & Mirel, 1999; Haubrich, 1993). Even in cases of schools that were not comprehensive, but specialized in vocational subjects, commercial studies, the arts, or some other field, urban high schools were sizable by national standards. They also tended to be somewhat culturally variegated. This was true even as these schools were affected by the development of the city and the spatial arrangement of various population groups. As a consequence, there was a tendency for high schools in the larger cities, where social differentiation was most pronounced, to result in somewhat diverse student populations. This even was evident in the Chicago study mentioned earlier; even if schools often were segregated by race, there was considerable variation in the social class backgrounds of students (Havighurst, 1964). Moreover, this certainly was true of the suburbs, particularly as these communities attracted ever-larger numbers of families with teenagers in the 1960s and 1970s.

As the overall size of high schools grew, they inevitably included larger numbers of working-class youth. This was a part of Conant's vision of a school that brought youth from various social classes and groups together. He believed that the high school should be a universal American institution, even though he did not feel everyone should study the same subjects. Statistical evidence points to the success of these arguments. As the number of adolescents grew in the 1950s and 1960s, high school enrollments climbed dramatically. This was a consequence both of the baby boom and improved rates of high school attendance (West, 1996). By the end of the 1950s, more than 80% of American teenagers attended high school, making it virtually a universal experience for the first time in American history (Angus & Mirel, 1999). This had a number of important consequences.

One was the fact that adolescents as a social group were segregated from the rest of society for a significant amount of time each week, through most of the year, in institutions where they constituted the vast majority of the population. Because of age grading and the differentiated structure of most high schools, they did not even have systematic contact with youth in different age groups, such as young adults over 18 or 19. This contributed to the development of what James S. Coleman (1961, 1965) described as the "adolescent society" in this period, based largely in the American high school. And this was an important component of what many observers of American life at the time referred to as the "youth culture" (Cohen, 1997).

The behavior of youth in the 1950s was not altogether unprecedented, of course. Similar patterns of association and exuberance had appeared on college campuses in the 1920s and in some high schools in the 1930s and 1940s. As historian Paula Fass (1977) has noted, these early manifestations of the youth culture revolved around dancing, dating, and a growing preoccupation with fashion and social status. The appearance of large concentrations of young people on fast-growing campuses in the 1920s made it possible for them to create a parallel social milieu, replete with its own rules and standards of behavior. As Fass observed, the youth culture defined itself in distinction to the adult world, professing nonconformity to the dominant mores of traditional institutions, but it also imposed its own forms of compliance to new values and sensibilities, often quite uncompromising. The postwar youth culture was similar, but cast on a much broader scale, and it was considerably more variegated. Embracing ever-larger portions of the adolescent population, it became divided into innumerable subcultures, each with its own set of values and norms of behavior. While the college youth of the 1920s had been a cultural curiosity, the teenagers of the 1950s and beyond would eventually become a major influence on the larger society.

High schools were a critical component of the development of this phenomenon. Coleman (1961) argued that the social world of high school adolescence was defined by status groups associated with different sorts of school activities. In general, he found that athletics played an especially important role in the social life of high school students, especially boys. Academic performance was less important, although it may have gained significance as students progressed through school. Other studies examined the influence of the larger youth culture, which was commercially directed by record companies, the radio, television and print media, and a host of other enterprises. As noted earlier, adolescents had preferred distinctive forms of music for several decades, and dancing had been popular with the rise of dating as a distinctive teenage activity in the 1920s and 1930s. After World War II, however, the scale of participation in such activities grew to become much larger (Palladino, 1996).

In the 1950s new forms of teenage entertainment came into being with the rapid rise of rock and roll music as a popular idiom. New dances came into play also, and youth culture became associated with a variety of new forms of consumption. Fast cars, cigarette smoking and alcohol, and the hint of sexual promiscuity came to represent the new youth culture, and to distinguish it from the clean-cut images of youth from earlier decades. Despite attempts at censorship, these images were spread through the media, including radio, the movies, and the increasingly ubiquitous television. It is doubtful that any more than a minority of youth actually engaged in such activities routinely; but even for those who did not, the idea of rebellion against adult mores exerted a powerful appeal (Gilbert, 1986). And it was an impulse that would exert even greater influence in the decades to follow.

If music and movies were important features of youth culture, clothing may have been even more important. High school students in earlier decades had dressed like miniature adults, with boys sporting coats and ties and girls wearing dresses or skirts. As the number of students in school increased, standards of dress began to be challenged. As one study of students in Milwaukee found, by the late 1950s high school students there had shed coats, ties, and dresses in favor of slacks, shirts, and sweaters (Haubrich, 1993). In the 1960s high school dress codes became a subject of student protests, and were eliminated in schools across the country. By the 1970s jeans and T-shirts were the norm in many schools, and adolescent tastes were becoming a major force in the world of adult fashion (Palladino, 1996). A budding students' rights movement, abetted by the Supreme Court's 1969 *Tinker* decision upholding the rights of students to wear anti-war armbands, aggressively resisted dress codes and other institutional efforts to limit self-expression (Zirkel, 1999). At about the same time there was a dramatic shift in sexual mores, with a corresponding change in teenage behavior. Rates of nonmarital sex among teenagers increased significantly in the early 1970s, jumping from less then 20% to more than a third. Sexuality became a prominent feature of popular culture, and a central aspect of the rapidly evolving high school–based adolescent society. By the latter 1970s there was a movement to make sex education a major element of the secondary curriculum (Chilman, 1978; Esman, 1990; Palladino, 1996).

All of these trends in youth culture coincided with the movement to consolidate and expand high schools across the country, which Conant had endorsed so ardently. The average size of public high schools more than doubled between 1950 and 1970, and these figures understate the size of high schools most students attended in these years, due to the large number of small rural districts with combined elementary-secondary schools. Ernest Boyer (1983) estimated the average enrollment at nearly 900. *High School and Beyond* data collected in the 1970s and 1980s indicate that the typical public high school at that time had some 875 students, and more than 40% had above 900 (Bryk, Lee, & Holland, 1993). It was the latter schools, of course, that enrolled most of the nation's metropolitan high school students, and they continue to do so today.

The biggest high schools historically were concentrated in urban areas, but many suburban districts also established large secondary schools as their teenage populations expanded rapidly in the postwar years. For metropolitan youth, the institutional norm became a large, differentiated public high school. On the question of school size, Conant's arguments appear to have won the day.

Ironically, the development of larger high schools, with greater numbers of students and psychological distance between adolescents and adults, may have enabled the development of this school-based youth culture. Barker and Gump (1964), in their analysis of high school size in the 1960s, found that greater numbers of students were excluded from school activities in larger schools, a condition that contributed to more widespread alienation from the institution. More recent research has associated a loss of adult control with larger schools, and a reduction in the degree of personalism in contact between students and adults. A number of studies have argued that greater school size inhibits student learning, especially when it makes it difficult for adolescents and adults to communicate meaningfully (Haller, 1992; Sizer, 1996). This point was made emphatically by scholars comparing private—particularly Catholic—and public high schools. These authors reported that school size was a significant factor in accounting for the superior academic performance and school climate of private institutions (Bryk, Lee, & Holland, 1993; Coleman, Hoffer, & Kilgore, 1982). Bigger, it turned out, was not always better.

This seems to have been especially true in big cities, in schools with large minority student populations (Lee & Smith, 1997; Meier, 1996), but it also was evident in suburban institutions. Pamela Bettis (1996) has described the lack of efficacy experienced by urban youth in large schools. Signithia Fordham (1996) has suggested that large all-black high schools engender a student culture of resistance to academic achievement; Paul Willis (1977) has observed a parallel subculture among working-class youth in Great Britain. In her perceptive analysis of student cultures in a suburban setting, *Jocks and Burnouts,* Penelope Eckert (1989) found a high level of disengagement among working-class youth, for whom the school had come to represent a point of negative reference. On the other hand, for some youth, there were positive experiences of identification with the schools and their academic mission. But the development of overt student cultures of "resistance" in such settings were observed to have been assisted by the very size of the schools. Indeed, Eckert has reported that opposition appeared to be less evident in smaller schools. There is considerable evidence, on the other hand, that smaller institutions—again, especially Catholic schools that foster a clear sense of community—have had greater success with urban students (Greeley, 1982). Conant's insistence on the need for larger schools, in that case, may have contributed to some of the most difficult problems faced by American secondary education in recent years. This was yet another irony of the comprehensive high school model of secondary education.

As Coleman and other observers have noted, youth culture often took the immediate community and its values as a point of departure. This accounted for the heavy value placed on athletics (Coleman, 1961). But with the social and economic differentiation of the metropolitan landscape, this has resulted in a variegated adolescent culture, or, alternatively, a set of youth subcultures (Coleman, 1965). This can be seen nationally in the highly fragmented forms of youth culture that came to exist in the popular media (Giroux, 1996). As suggested in Gerald Grant's (1988) poignant study of a single urban high school, conflict between various student subcultures became a major predicament of secondary education in the 1960s and afterward. If these varied elements of adolescent society perform a major element of the socialization that occurs in the large, differentiated metropolitan high schools of the latter 20th century, what has happened to Conant's vision of the high school as an agent of democratic socialization? This may be yet another aspect of how the comprehensive high school ideal that he represented has contributed to challenges facing secondary education as we approach a new century.

HIGH SCHOOLS, YOUTH, AND THE CHANGING URBAN ECONOMY

Another important facet of urban life that changed in the postwar period was the youth labor market. Early in the 20th century most American youth started to work before age 20, even if only on a part-time basis (Kett, 1977). Employment rates for high school–aged youth contracted dramatically in the 1930s, however, as a consequence of the Great Depression. This ended during World War II as demand for labor skyrocketed. By the postwar period the job market for youth had been restored somewhat, but patterns of high school enrollment established during the Depression also returned. More youth enrolled in high school meant that fewer took jobs than in earlier times (Angus & Mirel, 1999). And this also meant that the high school changed. Larger numbers of working-class youth entered the high school at this time, posing a challenge to the integrating function of Conant's comprehensive ideal.

The urban economy also changed profoundly in the decades following World War II. In the immediate postwar period, industrial jobs were plentiful, and it was the prospect of employment in the booming factories of the great Northern cities that drew African Americans out of the South in the 1950s. Despite periodic downturns, the urban-industrial economy was flush during the 1950s, but showed signs of change in the following decade (Teaford, 1990). By the mid-1960s some observers already were warning that the demand for unskilled labor would be limited in the future, even if their projections underestimated the rate of long-term change (Harrison, 1972; Havighurst, 1966). Few, however, anticipated the shifting relationship of education and employment that characterized the closing decades of the century.

The very idea of the comprehensive high school, of course, was premised on the principle of differentiation: the notion that high school youth are destined to enter a variety of different occupational fields upon graduation. This was in large part a legacy of the Progressive era, and the social efficiency rationale for the vocational education movement. The *Cardinal Principles* held that the high school should be preparation for life, and vocational education advocates argued that there were many different roads that students may take in their working careers. This was certainly true in the 1920s, when a smaller fraction of the high school–aged population attended school, even in the cities (Krug, 1972). And it continued to be true in the immediate postwar period. Industrial employment remained quite robust, and although many high school graduates did not find jobs as manual laborers, the rationale for vocational training was still clear (Coleman, 1965). As the urban economy changed, however, the relevance of vocationalism weakened. And vocational education became supplanted with a variety of other curricular options, but particularly with the "general course." Some historians have referred to this as "warehousing" (Angus & Mirel, 1999).

Even if the sectoral distribution of employment did not change in the short term, the economy was evolving in new ways and demanding new skills of entry-level workers. Literacy requirements in the workplace were rising, especially in the 1960s and 1970s, at the same time that the academic quality of urban high schools began to falter (Ginzberg, 1975; Levine & Zipp, 1993). In the wake of conflicting reform agendas, the national high school curriculum lost focus (Angus & Mirel, 1999; Rury, 2002).

This contributed to the crisis of urban education that unfolded in the 1970s and 1980s. And it was linked to the rising national interest in education reflected in the publication of *A Nation at Risk* in the early 1980s. In many cities employers expressed concern about the poor quality of inner-city high schools, and the difficulties they faced in finding capable workers. Such questions became more commonplace in the latter 1980s, as employment opportunities in downtown offices expanded rapidly in connection with the burgeoning banking, financial services, and insurance industries (Abu-Lughod, 1999; Levine & Trachtman, 1988). It was the dawn of a new era.

These changes were tied to a set of larger shifts in the American economy that have received much attention in recent years. During the time Conant wrote, *The American High School Today*, more than a quarter of all U.S. workers were employed in manufacturing. When employees in industry were added to other sectors of the economy requiring similar skills, over 40% of the labor force could be classified as blue collar, both skilled and unskilled. Another 35% were clerical workers, most of them employed in urban offices. On the other hand, managerial and professional employment accounted for less than a quarter of the nation's overall employment (Levy, 1987; Long, 1958). Given this, it appeared quite reasonable for Conant and others to surmise that the majority of American youth would not require education beyond the secondary level. For these students, vocational or commercial training would be most appropriate. Only a minority of the "brightest" youth need be prepared for postsecondary education (Conant, 1959, 1961).

The basic occupational structure of the American labor force changed slowly through the 1960s, with a gradual shift away from employment in manufacturing and greater numbers of workers in the "service sector." In 1970 more than a quarter of the nation's workers were employed in manufacturing, and the number of positions requiring higher education had changed relatively little. But the years that followed witnessed a dramatic transformation that continues to unfold today. Beginning in the 1970s, and accelerating in the decades that followed, the number of manufacturing jobs began to plummet (Levy, 1987). Nationwide, the proportion of the labor force employed in manufacturing fell from about a quarter to 18% between 1970 and 1990 (Murphy & Welch, 1993). The impact of this was evident first in the cities, as noted above, but eventually affected all areas of the country. Economists speculate that it was due both to technological change and to the movement of jobs to other countries (Abramovitz & David, 1996). And it was a set of changes that came to have important implications for schools. The number of jobs for which relatively little formal education was necessary had begun to contract.

Jobs in manufacturing were replaced by positions in offices, and by growth in management and technical and professional employment. This was slow to develop, but beginning in the 1980s a shift toward jobs requiring progressively higher levels of education had become evident (Cohn & Hughes, 1994; Murphy & Welch, 1989). This was reflected in wage rates for workers with different levels of education. At the start of the 1970s the hourly earnings for employees with less than a high school education and college graduates were about $7 apart, and high school graduates earned only about $1.50 more per hour than nongraduates. Because of the large cohort of college graduates produced in the 1960s and 1970s, the advantage of college actually shrank appreciably in the 1970s, and in 1979 only about $6 separated the hourly wages of high school dropouts and college graduates. But after that the gap began to widen, and by the mid-1990s college graduates earned nearly $10 more per hour than high school noncompleters, and more than seven dollars per hour than high school graduates (Datazone, 1999). In other words, the labor market began to pay even bigger returns to students who went to college.

This occurred because of two trends. First, dollar returns to college education increased slightly across the 1980s and 1990s, roughly 7%. At the same time, however, the wages of high school dropouts fell by more than a quarter, and those of high school graduates declined by about 8%. The impact on high school dropouts was particularly dramatic (Stern, 1989). Thus, by the 1990's the earnings premium for attending college was greater than at any time in the postwar period. This, not surprisingly, helped to spur a corresponding jump in college enrollments. Beginning in the mid-1980s, ever-larger numbers of American high school graduates entered college. While fewer than half of high school seniors continued on to college in the early 1980s, by the latter 1990s the figure approached 70% (Murphy & Welch, 1993). These choices by students, of course, were rational decisions, given the decline of employment opportunities for students without higher education, and the growing wage differentials. By 1990 it was calculated that a college degree was, on average, worth half a million dollars more than a high school diploma in lifetime earnings. Figures such as these helped to make the idea of attending college attractive to a much broader range of American youth than had been the case just two decades earlier (Hunt, 1995).

A dramatic rise in female labor force participation in the 1970s and 1980s also contributed to this general trend. Among the most rapidly growing areas of female employment were the professions, and other jobs requiring some measure of higher education. Consequently, female enrollments in college climbed sharply, particularly in the 1980s and 1990s. This was the case despite a lower responsiveness in female enrollments to wage dividends for college (Averett & Burton, 1996). By the final decade of the century, women substantially outnumbered men among undergraduates for the first time in American history. This contributed to the rapid rise in the number of high school graduates continuing on to college in the 1990s; indeed, the rate of college entry among women was about 10% greater than among men.

Across the country educational expectations were rising in the latter 20th century. In an analysis of white high school graduates in 1960 and 1980, Marlis Buchmann found that students' expectations of the highest degree they would earn changed significantly between these two cohorts. Altogether, the number expecting to simply end their education at high school fell from more than a quarter to just 18%, almost a 30% drop. At the same time, those expecting to earn graduate or advanced professional degrees increased from about 12% to over 21% (Buchmann, 1989). These trends would only accelerate in the years to follow.

Such changes in students' educational plans can be interpreted as a reasonable response to the changing job market. As Buchmann and a number of other observers have noted, the earning power of high school diplomas faded in the 1980s, at the same time that returns to college education began to increase significantly. This was partly due to shifts in the occupational structure, with the decline in manufacturing employment. But it was also due to the growing preference of employers to hire workers—especially beginning employees—with higher levels of education (Carnevale & Desrochers, 1997). In a thoughtful analysis of employment data, Kevin Murphy and Finis Welch (1993) have argued that the numbers of workers with a college education increased in all industrial sectors in the 1980s, contributing to a broad rising demand for higher levels of educational attainment. These changes helped to fuel a continuing expansion of the higher education sector, despite smaller numbers of high school graduates, through the latter 1980s and early 1990s. By the middle of the 1990s, a majority of high school graduates across the country were continuing on to some form or another of higher education.

With these dramatic shifts in the national economy, the stakes of educational decisions made by teenagers became quite high. Christopher Jencks and Meredith Phillips (1998) recently have found that future earnings were tied to skill levels measured by tests for cohorts born in the 1960s and 1970s, just when schools appear to have failed in large measure to effectively transmit the requisite skills. For students who did not develop their academic skills in high school and who chose not to continue on to some form of higher education, real wages declined in the decades following 1979. Given this, it is little wonder that enrollments in academic courses increased in this period. It was a reaction to the development of a new economic reality in metropolitan America.

The changing economy helped to underscore the importance of educational differences between inner-city and suburban communities. While the latter kept pace with the new expectations of the economy, the former fell farther behind (Harrison, 1972; Sexton & Nickel, 1992). For inner-city neighborhoods, and the students who live in them, the prospect of vocational education providing a means of economic development has faded. This was evident as early as the late 1970s, and was reported by Boyer in 1983. Today it is reflected somewhat in the improved rates of college enrollment for African Americans, but postsecondary participation rates for Hispanic students has lagged behind the advance of other groups in the past two decades. As the new service economy continues to develop in the years ahead, these patterns of educational differentiation could pose a significant problem.

Part of the difficulty with vocational education has been the rapid pace of change in the economy. This was a theme in Boyer's (1983) study of secondary education. In a more recent analysis of secondary vocational programs, John Bishop (1989) has argued that occupational education is least effective when it is not matched to existing jobs. As the number of central-city manufacturing jobs fell in the 1970s and 1980s, they were replaced by service positions, many of which required at least a high school diploma and a broad range of academic skills. A growing number of economists and other observers have suggested that computerization has allowed employers to replace low-skill jobs with more demanding positions (Katz, 2000; Murnane & Levy, 1996). And as the technical requirements of office jobs increased, many employers in the cities began to look for even higher educational credentials (Autor, Levy, & Murnane, 2002). One estimate suggests that as many as 52% of future jobs in metropolitan areas will require at least some college preparation (Dougherty, 1997). Youth without this background will clearly be at a disadvantage.

The emphasis today, as never before in recent history, is on academic skills, and this is evident in the behavior of employers (Sexton & Nickol, 1992; Stern, 1989; Wilson, 1995). The growing educational mismatch between the expectations of downtown employers and the preparation of city high school students was a major impetus behind urban school reform campaigns of the last decade. In Chicago it has led to Mayor Richard M. Daley assuming control of the public schools and instituting a series of changes aimed at restoring the public image of the system and raising test scores (Shipps, 1998; Wong et al., 1997). New York City's schools came under Mayor Michael Bloomberg's control in 2002. Leaders in other cities are considering similar interventions, even though it is not clear that long-term gains in academic achievement will result from such a reform strategy ("Chicago, a work in progress," 1999). The fates of hundreds of thousands of poor and minority central-city youth hang in the balance.

Conant and other advocates of the comprehensive high school believed that the allocation of students to various types of curricula would correspond to the demand for various skills in the labor market. The historical development of the economy and recent changes in high school enrollments have proven this view to be correct in certain respects. The picture that has emerged in the past 15 years, however, is somewhat different from the one Conant had envisioned in the late 1950s. In response to the controversies of the early 1980s, and particularly the publication of *A Nation at Risk*, academic requirements for graduation have been raised for the majority of high school students, and vocational curricula serve a shrinking minority. Studies of Catholic high schools have argued that their success has been partly due to their generally undifferentiated academic curriculum (Bryk, Lee, & Holland, 1993). Critics of the high school today argue that all students should be provided with a rigorous academic curriculum if they are to succeed in the economy of the future (Angus & Mirel, 1999). If that vision comes to pass, it is a legitimate question whether the comprehensive high school envisioned by Conant would be necessary at all.

CONCLUSION

A number of historical developments converged in the decades following World War II to make James Conant's vision of the high school problematic, at least in the nation's large metropolitan areas. Racial segregation and the movement of Southern blacks to Northern cities divided urban and suburban school districts, creating sharp disparities in educational resource allocation and curricular orientation. Where Conant had imagined the comprehensive high school as an instrument of democratic socialization, by the 1970s it had evolved into an agency of racial isolation and alienation, at least in many metropolitan settings. Rather than bringing students from the nation's principal social/ethnic groups together, in certain respects high schools helped to highlight their differences.

This process was rooted in patterns of residential segregation, of course, but was encouraged by the emergence of a youth culture that also became fragmented along racial and social class lines. Conant's insistence on the importance of large schools may have helped to compromise adult authority in the face of the growing influence of the youth culture. The relaxation of rules and changing standards of conduct helped make the schools into centers of an elaborate social world for adolescent youth, diverting energy and enthusiasm from academic interests. Even if Conant was not a proponent of many of the reforms in student life, his campaign for larger schools helped to set the stage for other developments in the development of a school-based "adolescent society" in the postwar period.

Finally, changes in the economy altered the very premise of a differentiated curriculum for the high school. Conant already had noted the heavily academic orientation of suburban high schools in the 1960s. Two decades later this tendency became even more pronounced, as ever-larger numbers of high school graduates entered college of one sort or another. The rationale for vocational education became weaker as the manufacturing sector of the economy stagnated or even disappeared, as it had in many larger cities by the 1980s. In the last decade of the century, high schools across the country were offering stronger academic programs to all students. In the face of significant change in the economy and the rapidly rising value of academic skills, the academic curriculum was not suitable for only the most gifted students. The old comprehensive high school has been acquiring an increasingly academic demeanor.

At the end of the 20th century, few observers discuss the high school as an instrument for bringing students from different backgrounds together. Smaller schools are being urged to give educators greater authority and diminish the influence of the youth culture, in all of its varied manifestations; and the differentiated curriculum is giving way to a greater interest in academic preparation, driven in large part by changes in the economy and public perceptions about the importance of education, especially at the postsecondary level (Marsh & Codding, 1999). Given this, it may be the case that the age of the comprehensive high school is drawing to a close. James Conant, it seems, was wrong about the development of secondary education in the decades following publication of *The American High School Today*.

But observations such as these leave a numberns unanswered. What is the best institutional arrangement for the great variety of American youth to be educated in the coming century? Surely there will be a need for some occupational training, even if secondary education becomes more uniformly academic in orientation. Charles Benson (1997) has written about a "new vocationalism" that integrates academic and occupational curricula, and combines schoolwork with work-based learning, overcoming the disjunctures that often exist between schools and the labor market. Other observers suggest that intermediate postsecondary institutions, particularly community colleges, have a vital role to play in linking metropolitan youth to the rapidly changing job market (Grubb, 1995). Whatever the accommodations to the labor force, however, there is also the question of the high school's role in contributing to the democratic ethos of American society. At the same time that the institution's role in curricular differentiation seems to have diminished somewhat, its role in augmenting social and cultural distinctions in society appears to have grown larger. If James Conant were alive today, it is easy to speculate that he would find this a most troubling development. And it is difficult to see how anyone who is concerned with the long-term development of American civilization could disagree.

REFERENCES

Abramovitz, M., & David, P. A. (1996). Technological change and the rise of intangible investments: The U.S. economy's growth-path in the twentieth century. In OECD Documents, *Employment and growth in the knowledge-based economy* (pp. 35–60). Paris, France: Organization for Economic Cooperation and Development.

Abu-Lughod, J. (1999). *New York, Chicago, Los Angeles: America's global cities.* Minneapolis: University of Minnesota Press.

Angus, D., & Mirel, J. (1999). *The failed promise of the American high school, 1890–1995.* New York: Teachers College Press.

Autor, D. H., Levy, F., & Murnane, R. J. (2002). Upstairs, downstairs: Computers and skills on two floors of a large bank. *Industrial & Labor Relations Review, 55*(3), 432–447.

Averett, S. L., &. Burton, M. I. (1996). College attendance and the college wage premium: Differences by gender. *Economics of Education Review, 15*(1), 37–49.

Barker, R. G., & Gump, P. V. (1964). *Big school small school.* Stanford, CA: Stanford University Press.

Benson, C. (1997). New vocationalism in the United States: Potential problems and outlook. *Economics of Education Review, 16*(3), 201–212.

Bettis, P. J. (1996). Urban students, liminality, and the postindustrial context. *Sociology of Education, 69*(2), 105–125.

Bishop, J. (1989). Occupational training in high school: When does it pay off? *Economics of Education Review, 8*(1), 1–15.

Boyer, E. L. (1983). *High school: A report on secondary education in America.* New York: Harper & Row.

Bryk, A., Lee, V. E., & Holland, P. B. (1993). *Catholic schools and the common good.* Cambridge, MA: Harvard University Press.

Buchmann, M. (1989). *The script of life in modern society: Entry into adulthood in a changing world.* Chicago: University of Chicago Press.

Carnevale, A. P., & Desrochers, D. M. (1997). The role of the community college in the new economy: Spotlight on education. *Community College Journal, 67*(5), 26–33.

Chicago Assembly. (1998). *Educational reform for the 21st century.* Chicago: Harris Graduate School of Public Policy.

Chicago, a work in progress: For schools, it's only a start. (1999, February 12). *The Chicago Tribune*, pp. 1, 13.

Chilman, C. S. (1978). *Adolescent sexuality in a changing American society: Social and psychological perspectives.* Washington, D.C.: U.S. Government Printing Office.

Cohen, R. (1997). The delinquents: Censorship and youth culture in recent U.S. history. *History of Education Quarterly, 37*(3), 251–270.

Cohn, E., & Hughes, W. W. (1994). A benefit-cost analysis of investment in college education in the United States, 1969–1985. *Economics of Education Review, 13*(2), 109–123.

Coleman, J. S. (1961). *The adolescent society: The social life of the teenager and its impact on education.* Glencoe: The Free Press.

Coleman, J. S. (1965). *Adolescents and the schools.* New York: Basic Books.

Coleman, J. S., Hoffer, T., & Kilgore, S. (1982). *High school achievement: Public, Catholic and private schools compared.* New York: Basic Books.

Commission on the Reorganization of Secondary Education. (1918). *Cardinal principles of secondary education.* Washington, D.C.: U.S. Bureau of Education, Bulletin #35.

Conant, J. B. (1959). *The American high school today: A first report to interested citizens.* New York: McGraw-Hill.

Conant, J. B. (1961). *Slums and suburbs: A commentary on schools in metropolitan areas.* New York: McGraw-Hill.

Cremin, L. A. (1961). *Transformation of the school: Progressivism in American education, 1876–1957.* New York: Alfred Knopf.

Datazone, The. (1999). *Average real hourly wages of all workers by education, 1973–1997.* http://epinet.org/datazone/wagebyed_all.html.

Dougherty, K. J. (1997). Mass higher education: What is its impetus? What is its impact? *Teachers College Record, 99*(1), 66–72.

Eckert, P. (1989). *Jocks and burnouts: Social categories and identity in the high school.* New York: Teachers College Press.

Esman, A. H. (1990). *Adolescence and culture.* New York: Columbia University Press.

Fass, P. S. (1977). *The damned and the beautiful: American youth in the 1920's.* New York: Oxford University Press.

Fordham, S. (1996). *Blacked out: Dilemmas of race, identity and success at capitol high.* Chicago: University of Chicago Press.

Fox, K. (1985). *Metropolitan America: Urban life and urban policy in the United States, 1940–1980.* New Brunswick, NJ: Rutgers University Press.

Gilbert, J. B. (1986). *A cycle of outrage: America's response to the juvenile delinquent of the 1950s.* New York: Oxford University Press.

Ginzberg, E. (1975). *The manpower connection: Education and work.* Cambridge, MA: Harvard University Press.

Giroux, H. (1996). *Fugitive cultures: Race, violence and youth.* New York: Routledge

Goldsmith, W. W., & Blakely, E. J. (1992). *Separate societies: Poverty and inequality in U.S. cities.* Philadelphia: Temple University Press.

Grant, G. (1988). *The world we created at Hamilton High*. Cambridge, MA: Harvard University Press.

Greeley, A. (1982). *Catholic schools and minority students*. New Brunswick, NJ: Transaction Books.

Grubb, N. (1995). Postsecondary education and the sub-baccalaureate labor market: Corrections and extensions. *Economics of Education Review, 14*(3), 285–299.

Haller, E. J. (1992). High school size and student indiscipline: Another aspect of the school consolidation issue? *Educational Evaluation and Policy Analysis, 14*(2), 145–156.

Hampel, R. L. (1986). *The last little citadel: American high schools since 1940*. Boston: Houghton Mifflin.

Harrison, B. (1972). *Education, training and the urban ghetto*. Baltimore: Johns Hopkins University Press.

Haubrich, P. (1993). Student life in Milwaukee high schools, 1920–1985. In J. L. Rury & F. A. Cassell (Eds.), *Seeds of crisis: Public schooling in Milwaukee since 1920* (pp. 193–228). Madison: University of Wisconsin Press.

Havighurst, R. (1964). *The public schools of Chicago: A survey for the Board of Education of the City of Chicago*. Chicago: Board of Education of the City of Chicago.

Havighurst, R. (1966). *Education in metropolitan areas*. Boston: Allyn and Bacon.

Hawes, J. M., & Hiner, N. R. (1985). *American childhood: A research guide and handbook*. Westport, CT: Greenwood Press.

Herbst, J. (1996). *The once and future school: Three hundred and fifty years of American secondary education*. New York: Routledge.

Hochschild, J. (1985). *The new American dilemma: Liberal democracy and school desegregation*. New Haven, CT: Yale University Press.

Hunt, E. (1995). *Will we be smart enough? A cognitive analysis of the coming workforce*. New York: Rusell Sage Foundation.

Jackson, K. (1985). *The crabgrass frontier: The suburbanization of the United States*. New York: Oxford University Press.

Jencks, C., & Phillips, M. (1998). The black-white test score gap: An introduction. In C. Jencks & M. Phillips (Eds.), *The black-white test score gap* (pp. 1–51). Washington, D.C.: The Brookings Institution.

Kantor, H., & Brenzel, B. (1993). Urban education and the 'Truly Disadvantaged': The historical roots of the contemporary crisis, 1945–1990. In M. B. Katz (Ed.), *The underclass debate: Views from history* (pp. 366–401). Princeton, NJ: Princeton University Press.

Katz, L. F. (2000). Technological change, computerization, and the wage structure. In E. Brynjolfsson & B. Kahin (Eds.), *Understanding the digital economy: Data, tools, and research* (pp. 217–244). Cambridge, MA, and London: MIT Press.

Kett, J. (1977). *Rites of passage: A history of youth and adolescence in America*. New York: Harper.

Kleppner, P. (1984). *Chicago divided: The making of a Black mayor*. DeKalb: Northern Illinois University Press.

Kozol, J. (1991). *Savage inequalities: Children in America's schools.* New York: Crown Publishers.

Krug, E. A. (1972). *The American high school, 1920–1940.* Madison: University of Wisconsin Press.

Lee, V., & Smith, J. (1997). High school size: Which works best and for whom? *Educational Evaluation and Policy Analysis, 19*(3), 205–227.

Levine, M., & Trachtman, R. (1988). *American business and the public schools: Case studies of corporate involvement in public education.* New York: Teachers College Press.

Levine, M., & Zipp, J. F. (1993). A city at risk: The changing social and economic context of public schooling in Milwaukee. In J. L. Rury & F. A. Cassell (Eds.), *Seeds of crisis: Public schooling in Milwaukee since 1920* (pp. 42–73). Madison: University of Wisconsin Press.

Levy, F. (1987). *Dollars and dreams: The changing American income distribution.* New York: The Russell Sage Foundation.

Long, C. D. (1958). *The labor force under changing income and employment.* Princeton, NJ: Princeton University Press.

Marsh, D. D., & Codding, J. (1999). *The new American high school.* Thousand Oaks, CA: Corwin Press.

Massey, D., & Denton, N. (1993). *American apartheid: Segregation and the making of the underclass.* Cambridge, MA: Harvard University Press.

Meier, D. (1996). Supposing that. . . . *Phi Delta Kappan, 78*(4), 271–276.

Mirel, J. (1993). *The rise and fall of an urban school system: Detroit, 1907–81.* Ann Arbor: University of Michigan Press.

Mora, M. T. (1997). Attendance, schooling quality, and the demand for education of Mexican Americans, African Americans, and non-Hispanic Whites. *Economics of Education Review, 16*(4), 407–418.

Murnane, R. J., & Levy, F. (1996). *Teaching the new basic skills: Principles for educating children to thrive in a changing economy.* New York: The Free Press.

Murphy, K. M., & Welch, F. (1989). Wage premiums for college graduates: Recent growth and possible explanations. *Educational Researcher, 18*(4), 17–26.

Murphy, K. M., & Welch, F. (1993). Industrial change and the importance of skill. In S. Danziger & P. Gottschalk, *Uneven Tides: Rising Inequality in America* (pp. 101–132). New York: Russell Sage Foundation.

Orfield, G. (1978). *Must we bus? Segregated schools and national policy.* Washington, D.C.: The Brookings Institution.

Orfield, G., Eaton, S., & the Harvard Project on School Desegregation. (1996). *Dismantling desegregation: The quiet reversal of Brown v. Board of Education.* New York: The New Press.

Palen, J. J. (1992). *The urban world* (4th ed.). New York: McGraw Hill.

Palladino, G. (1996). *Teenagers: An American history.* New York: Basic Books.

Rumberger, R., & Willms, D. J. (1992). The impact of racial and ethnic segregation on the achievement gap in California high schools. *Educational Evaluation and Policy Analysis, 14*(4), 377–396.

Rury, J. (1999). Race, space and the politics of Chicago's public schools: Benjamin

Willis and the tragedy of urban education. *History of Education Quarterly,* *39*(2), 117–142.

Rury, J. (2002). Democracy's high school? Social change and American secondary education in the post-Conant era. *American Educational Research Journal,* *39*(2), 307–336.

Sexton, E., & Nickel, J. F. (1992). The effects of school location on the earnings of Black and White youths. *Economics of Education Review,* *11*(1), 11–18.

Shipps, D. (1998). Corporate influences on Chicago school reform. In C. Stone (Ed.), *Changing urban education* (pp. 161–183). Lawrence: University Press of Kansas.

Sizer, T. (1996). New hope for high schools. *American School Board Journal,* *183*(9), 37–40.

Stern, D. (1989). Labor market experience of teenagers with and without high school diplomas. *Economics of Education Review, 8*(3), 233–246.

Stolee, M. (1993). The Milwaukee desegregation case. In J. L. Rury & F. A. Cassell (eds.), *Seeds of crisis: Public schooling in Milwaukee since 1920* (pp. 229–268). Madison: University of Wisconsin Press.

Stone, C. N. (1998). Introduction. In C. Stone (Ed.), *Changing urban education* (pp. 1–20). Lawrence: University Press of Kansas.

Teaford, J. C. (1990). *Rough road to renaissance: Urban revitalization in America, 1940–1985.* Baltimore: Johns Hopkins University Press.

Wells, A. S., & Crain, R. L. (1997). *Stepping over the color line: African American students in White suburban schools.* New Haven, CT: Yale University Press.

West, E. (1996). *Growing up in twentieth-century America: A history and reference guide.* Westport, CT: Greenwood Press.

Willis, P. (1977). *Learning to labor.* New York: Routledge.

Wilson, W. J. (1987). *The truly disadvantaged: The inner city, the underclass, and public policy.* Chicago: University of Chicago Press.

Wilson, W. J. (1995). *When work disappears: The world of the new urban poor.* New York: Alfred A. Knopf.

Wong, K., Dreeben, R. L., Sunderman, L., & Sunderman, G. (1997). *Integrated governance as a school reform strategy in the Chicago public schools.* Chicago: Department of Education and Harris Graduate School of Public Policy Studies, University of Chicago.

Zirkel, P. A. (1999). The thirtieth anniversary of "Tinker." *Phi Delta Kappan, 81,* 34–40.

4

Democratic Spirit and Moral Learning in Comprehensive High Schools

ROGER SHOUSE

For James Conant, "comprehensiveness" represented a critical organizational characteristic of American high schools, one that linked our nation's belief in democratic principles with its increasing need for well-trained citizen-workers (Conant, 1964). Through comprehensiveness, schools could break down artificial forms of social stratification, promote social mobility and equity, and produce the scientific and scholarly talent necessary for the nation's social, economic, and military security. In short, comprehensive high schools could generate an amalgam of democracy and human capital. Accomplishing this, however, would require attracting a student body large enough to permit regular offerings of high-status academic curricula and diverse enough to permit formal and informal interaction between students from a range of backgrounds, abilities, and future career paths.

Conant used the term "democratic spirit" to describe both the organizational quality that would emerge from such a setting as well as the enduring characteristics that schools could convey to students by training and shaping their intellect and attitudes. His argument of a linkage between school comprehensiveness and democratic spirit appears to chafe, however, against some popular current thinking about schools. It is frequently argued, for example, that large "bureaucratic" high schools are responsible for lower student achievement, academic and social disengagement, and lower levels of educational equality across lines of race and ethnicity. In addition, large size is said to impede a school's ability to foster personalistic relationships, collegial spirit, and the extended teacher role necessary for influencing student intellect and attitude (Bryk & Driscoll, 1988; Lee & Smith, 1995). For many supporters of the move toward smaller, more communal schools, Conant's argument must seem at best naïve, at worst elitist.

The purpose of this chapter, however, is to explore whether Conant's critics, and critics of larger schools generally, have overlooked some intriguing and compelling theoretical connections between comprehensive schooling and the emergence of a sense of democratic spirit among high school youth. Specifically, I will examine how large size and comprehensiveness may actually help schools offer a wider range of informal, semiformal, and formal experiences from which students can acquire such spirit. In fact, many of the links to be discussed here seem to have been largely overlooked by Conant, who focused mainly on the formal structures of high schools. At the same time, the chapter also highlights how size and comprehensiveness can threaten certain pathways to students' acquisition of democratic spirit and suggest ways in which schools can respond to these threats.

At the outset, however, three provisos are necessary. The first is that comprehensiveness is not necessarily incompatible with the goal of having students attend smaller, more communal schools. Indeed, Conant (1959) speculated that the potential for comprehensiveness was threatened only as the size of a school's graduating class dropped toward 100 students. The second proviso is that whatever benefits larger, more comprehensive schools can deliver in terms of shaping students' sense of democratic spirit, these probably decrease and disappear entirely when schools become extremely large. For example, urban high schools with populations in the 3,000-to-5,000 range may for all practical purposes become socially unmanageable, at least from any democratic or humanistic point of view. Finally, to highlight how democratic spirit is imparted in larger high schools is not tantamount to criticizing the capabilities of smaller, more communal schools to accomplish the same task. Rather, I would suggest that small and large schools accomplish the task in different ways, thus generating different "flavors" of democratic spirit and moral learning.

THE MEANING OF "DEMOCRATIC SPIRIT"

Conant's conception of democratic spirit ties school organizational qualities to students' moral and intellectual character, and these to larger national sociopolitical and socioeconomic characteristics. At this larger social level, Conant highlights America's sense of social equality and mutual respect; its ability to produce the world's best minds, ideas, and products; and its citizens' ability, desire, and opportunity to contribute toward all of these ends. But to generate this kind of social ethos, the school must accomplish two contrasting tasks. It must create and expand pathways for advanced academic talent while also conveying the message that for many students, less rigorous alternative paths are also worthy of pursuit. From Conant's perspective, comprehensive high schools manage these tasks in three ways:

1. By offering a program of challenging academic courses and by removing structural barriers to the development of academic talent, the school creates and expands a social current of intellectual activity.
2. Through curricular diversity and by allowing vertical and horizontal mobility across curricular categories, schools create flexible alternative paths for students to develop intellectual, vocational, and aesthetic skill, and to attain social status based on their own personal talents and interests.
3. By creating opportunities for interaction between students of different backgrounds, interests, and abilities (i.e., the use of homerooms and heterogeneous civics classes), schools reduce artificial social barriers and antagonisms, thereby promoting mutual understanding and respect.

Conant thus viewed democratic spirit as primarily an organizational characteristic, one expected to have long-term effects on students and the society they would eventually join. This is fine, as far as it goes, but some problems seem apparent. The first is Conant's relative silence regarding what democratic spirit actually looks like in students and young adults. What distinguishes this special civic attitude from other related qualities such as being academically talented, having a good job, being effective in one's job, or generally becoming integrated into adult society? In addition, Conant's vision seem to leave us with another "black box"—it offers organizational parameters and describes some social outcomes, but is largely implicit about the mechanisms by which schools imbue students with a sense of democratic spirit. Related to this, with its emphasis on formal organizational structures, Conant is largely silent regarding how democratic understandings are transmitted (or impeded) through less formal, less structured social interactions outside the formal curriculum.

HOW IS DEMOCRATIC SPIRIT REVEALED IN STUDENTS?

The overarching question here, of course, is that of how schools actually influence students' understandings about democratic life. Tackling this question requires us to forge some working student-level definition of democratic spirit. Taking a rudimentary stab at this, I will suggest that democratic spirit is revealed as students maintain, attach appropriate meanings to, and act based on a "classically liberal" moral and ethical code. This means that to acquire a sense of democratic spirit, one must first develop a conceptual framework of meaning connecting the key ideas of American democracy—"justice," "equality," "freedom," "fairness," "tolerance," "respect for others," and so forth. Gradually, over the duration of one's schooling, this framework must come to fit within the range of belief that Americans are willing to accept under their democratic tent. In general, this range is anchored by Jefferson's Declaration of Independence. It runs between Allen Bloom's (1987) notions of "democratic man" and "democratic personality," from an emphasis on natural rights to one of maximized freedom for individuals. Finally, of course, belief must be manifest in some action—as subtle as voting or donating money to a civic cause, or as obvious as speaking at a town meeting or joining in a political demonstration.

Needless to say, some ambiguity remains here. People on opposing sides of the abortion issue, for example, may attach very different meaning to the concept of "individual freedom" and, accordingly, act in very different ways. But as long as they refrain from violent or repressive acts against each other, members of both camps fall within the range of meaning described above (even, ironically, as they try to portray each other as "outside the democratic tent"). We may view peaceful demonstration or even civil disobedience as acts of democratic spirit. But no matter how peaceful, few would apply that designation to activities of totalitarian or fascist groups.

Based on his own words and those he cites from the *Cardinal Principles of Secondary Education* (Commission on the Reorganization of Secondary Education, 1918), Conant (1959, 1964) recognized that schools must influence young people in the ways suggested above, that they must prepare students to advance and reshape society, not merely find a useful place in it. For the greater part of this century American public schooling has accepted this challenge mostly through curricular reforms such as those advanced by the *Cardinal Principals,* by Conant, and by numerous others.

But structured academic activity represents only part of the mechanism by which schools transmit key moral and ethical concepts and meanings. For example, extracurricular activities, though part of the formal organization of schools, offer students wide opportunity for informal and semistructured interaction and engagement. Moral learning is also shaped by the varied social interactions and events of school life unfolding at or beyond the margins of teacher control and organizational structure. Though Conant was largely silent on such informal sources of democratic spirit, they seem rather important to his case. Specifically, to what extent might comprehensiveness (or other school characteristics such as communality or small size) enhance or constrain the informal transmission of democratic spirit?

SOURCES OF DEMOCRATIC LEARNING

First of all, it is important to note that the school is just one of many influences on students' moral and ethical learning. Other formal institutions (family, church, scouts) and educative channels (television, film, music) often shape these to an even greater degree. Second, students acquire democratic meaning formally (that is, via explicit lessons constructed for them by others—parents, teachers, various print and electronic media) as well as informally (via life experience, social interaction, implicit media messages). Third, to the extent schools do contribute to the development of democratic understanding, they do so in both formal and informal ways. This occurs formally via explicit instruction, rules and sanctions, and class projects, for example. Informally, it occurs by virtue of the fact that having gathered large numbers of young people together for a substantial portion of their lives, schools create a setting for authentic moral and ethical drama to unfold. Between these two extremes, schools offer the opportunity for a great deal of semistructured interaction through clubs, teams, and other kinds of extracurricular activities.

These points are highlighted by briefly sketching out some of the ways young children begin to develop key moral, ethical, and democratic concepts through formal and informal means both in and out of school. Formal avenues include parents' explicit lessons and messages, as well as explicit messages from television (*Mister Rogers' Neighborhood, Barney and Friends,* or, in my time, *Romper Room*). Informally, a very young child may conceive the possibility of fairness or justice by experiencing an authentic "moral event." A parent punishes him "unfairly." A neighbor shouts, "Please stop running through my yard!" The man at the drugstore won't give him a nickel (two cents in my time) for a dirty pop bottle he found. Sometimes the lessons are more serious. In his neighborhood he encounters a devious bully one day, an honest friend the next. Gradually, he learns something about trust—when to give it, when to withhold it, and the risks of making a mistake.

Later on, students experience similar kinds of formal and informal social lessons in school. Formally, teachers stress the importance of honesty and fair play and explain why it's wrong to steal or cheat. Each observance of a teacher enforcing or failing to enforce a classroom rule adds another plank to a student's moral and ethical understanding. Understanding is also reinforced through instructional content. Fables, myths, legends, and true stories convey what can happen when people struggle to live up to (or fail to live up to) noble personal and social ideals. Other formal, structured avenues for social understanding include directed projects that extend beyond the classroom, which lead the child to "realize the social scene of action" (Dewey, 1909/1975, p. 31).

Although much attention is focused on the formal ways schools contribute to students' moral development, their informal contributions tend to be underestimated or overlooked in schools' literature (they receive much more attention in popular television and film). School hallways, lunchrooms, and playing fields have always served as real-life laboratories for students to observe moral events, make choices, and learn from the choices they and others make. Someone finds a wallet full of money and must decide what to do. In turn, this may set off ripples of further moral activity. Other students begin talking about what should be done. At least one child will say "finder's keepers, loser's weepers," at least one other will challenge the slogan, and further argument will ensue. If the finder decides to keep the money, other students may wrestle with their own consciences. Some will bring the story home, thus allowing parents to offer guidance. A student may report losing a wallet; another may tell a teacher that someone found one. Such patterns of activity represent a miniature, if you will, "embryonic" version of the kinds of moral activity that occur on a more complex and sophisticated basis in larger society. Moreover, like the explicit instructional dimension of schooling, these patterns themselves become more complex and sophisticated as students pass from childhood through adolescence.

Of course, I use the term "embryonic" to draw a connection between the informal moral dimension of schooling and Dewey's view of how schools could best transmit critical intellectual content and moral understandings. In Dewey's vision (1909/1975), this occurs to the extent that schools are able to reproduce "typical conditions of social life" (p. 14). In other words, through experience with authentic socially situated problems, students not only gain knowledge of science, math, history, mechanics, or art, but also learn how to live in a democratic community. But while Dewey's vision relies heavily on formal structured activity, an important share of school social life is shaped largely by students' informal organization. That is to say that a great deal of student social activity and learning unfolds at the margins of formal control, much in the same fashion as such activity and learning occur in our larger society.

Some theorists implicitly recognize this idea, that school life is rich with moral events and dilemmas. Lawrence Kohlberg's concept of the school as a "just community," for example, holds that this richness can be marshaled by and integrated into formal school structure so as to develop student moral thinking and democratic decisionmaking (Power, Higgins, & Kohlberg, 1989). Teachers may use a rule-making exercise to engage students in a discussion of why particular rules are needed and to help decentralize the responsibility for upholding the rules they make (Power, 1997). On a larger scale, schools have implemented "town hall" decisionmaking bodies where students and teachers consider problems and enact rules (Lightfoot, 1983; Sommers, 1984). Ostensibly, such activities provide not only a link between the informal and formal aspects of student life in school, but also authentic experience in democratic life.

But it's far from clear that schools must involve students in formal decisionmaking in order to provide an authentic democratic social setting. A former student of mine, a local high school teacher, recently related a story that illustrates this point. Because of size constraints, his school's ninth graders were required to attend classes in a separate building from their older classmates. After a significant number of ninth graders became upset at being excluded from various upper-class activities, a large group of them staged a sit-in in the school cafeteria. Teachers and administrators responded by creating a "teachable moment"—they talked to the students about civil disobedience and how it had been used historically. They reminded them that to engage in the practice was to assume the risk of lawful consequences (in this case, suspension from school) and that other avenues could be used to settle their complaint. After about an hour, most of the students had returned to class, and those who didn't were suspended for one day. What is fascinating about this entire process was how it represented a complex exchange of information, messages, and symbols critical to the growth of democratic meaning. While the school conveyed its authority and the price of resistance, students conveyed a message that resistance was possible, even noble, and that authorities might pay a price for not taking their concerns seriously.

What I describe here constitutes a valuable authentic tension in school. It is a tension that is probably threatened not just when schools severely restrict student freedom and decisionmaking authority, but also when they allow students a very large share of these. Offering an example of the latter problem, Christina Hoff Sommers (1984) described one high school's experiment with a Kohlberg-inspired "town hall" decisionmaking body. Over time, she reports, students voted to allow Walkman-style radios, to prohibit surprise quizzes and homework during vacation periods, and to institute a procedure by which teachers who assigned work deemed "too demanding" could be brought before a school "Fairness Board," an arrangement that according to Sommers caused teachers to feel "harassed and manipulated." Rather than devote their limited time and energy to reshaping student attitudes, teachers gradually withdrew from the process altogether. While some may view this as a case of students receiving experience in true democratic action, I would argue that they received a misleading and counterproductive impression about American democratic life.

By highlighting the less formal, less structured ways in which students develop democratic spirit, my intent is not to deemphasize the importance of more formal mechanisms such as rules, course content, or curricular organization. Instead, my purpose is to call attention to a question that cuts against some of the "small is beautiful" thinking in schools literature. Specifically, to what extent might students' development of democratic spirit be enhanced by the social looseness of larger, more comprehensive high schools? The next section focuses on how informal organizational elements can promote or inhibit the growth of democratic spirit, drawing particular contrasts between "small communal" and "large comprehensive" high schools.

ORGANIZATIONAL DIFFERENCES AND THE TRANSMISSION OF DEMOCRATIC SPIRIT

For two decades, much research has focused on the question of what impact school size and bureaucratic organization have on student achievement and attitudes toward school. Although some key studies examine the separate impact of these two variables, they often get lumped together, so as to contrast the "large bureaucratic" with the "small communal" model of schooling. The argument is often made that smaller size provides the conditions necessary for schools to have a more pervasive and enduring impact on students. These conditions include a set of common values, a shared agenda of activity, and an expanded caring role for teachers (Bryk & Driscoll, 1988). Larger high schools, it is argued, are much more prone to value uncertainty, diffuse activity, and impersonalistic relationships between adults and students. Along these lines, the comprehensive high school has received harsh criticism from school reform advocates as being socially disengaging and antidemocratic (see Wraga, 1999, for a summary of and response to a range of criticisms).

A good deal of this criticism, however, often seems driven by a set of particular beliefs as to the nature of effective schooling and as to the nature of democracy itself. For example, for critics who find many "traditional" school and classroom practices ineffective or undemocratic, comprehensiveness and large school size are viewed as barriers to systematic structural reform. In other words, I suspect that some critics might overlook the size and curricular expansiveness of a "shopping mall" high school were it to incorporate such characteristics as team teaching, heterogeneous grouping, cooperative learning, and "alternative" forms of student assessment. The point here is not to debate the merits of such practices, but simply to suggest that another, more traditional yet equally legitimate vision of schooling exists, one that is in many ways highly congruent with life in American capitalist democracy and that can be enhanced by school size and comprehensiveness.

The remaining paragraphs thus focus on how size and comprehensiveness work to both expand and impede student social engagement and sense of democratic spirit. In particular, the discussion will highlight how three school organizational elements influence the informal semistructured dimension of student social and moral learning. These elements are (1) organizational complexity, (2) boundary permeability, and (3) the trend toward bureaucratic and legalistic policies. The first of these, social complexity, lends support to much of Conant's view as to the democratizing influence of comprehensive high schools. The latter two elements, largely unanticipated by Conant, pose serious threats to democratic spirit by upsetting the balance between key informal and formal aspects of the school organization: boundary permeability by increasing the power of external norms and values to reshape school goals, bureaucracy and legalism by increasing the school's power over its members, thereby damaging its ability to distribute justice and moral authority.

Organizational Complexity

The following contrasts, though a bit stereotypical, illustrate the different normative mechanisms at play in small and large high schools. On one hand, a small private religious high school, through its rules, curriculum, and pervasive set of organizational norms, can have a very strong formal influence over students' moral and ethical learning and behavior. And yet, to the degree that such schools tend to attract families with congruent preexisting beliefs and behaviors, "control" or "maintenance" may be better words than "influence" in describing this process. While the school's small size may facilitate formal control, small size and formal control structures may also lead to fewer opportunities for the less structured, more authentic kinds of social interaction and eventfulness described earlier. A large comprehensive public high school, on the other hand, may have a weaker formal influence because of its more diffuse curriculum and control structure. But the potential for shaping student democratic spirit may be quite high due to the diversity of students' backgrounds and the greater opportunity for informal and authentic moral activity.

In the case of the small religious school, moral education and civic spirit emerge from the school performing in communitarian fashion. Norms and boundaries are well defined, and there is a strong sense of mutual obligation and responsibility. In the case of the larger comprehensive high school, moral and civic learning unfold in a more libertarian fashion. The school operates not so much as a single community, but more like a small city with multiple communities and institutions. Boundaries are permeable, norms compete and evolve, and there is an air of social uncertainty and often one of tolerance.

The social complexity and social looseness described above represent a critical, though implicit, element of Conant's vision of democratic ethos in comprehensive high schools. The connection becomes even more evident if we consider student social status within schools. In smaller, less complex school settings students must often grapple with a social structure that tends to be simple, visible, and fairly rigid, often defined largely in terms of one's academic standing, general popularity, or athletic ability in one of the few sports the school may offer. Larger schools, however, will tend to offer a greater number of opportunities for students to gain social status, a wider array of courses, athletic activities, clubs, and a multiplicity of social groups or "cliques" with which students may identify.

Though not specifically applied to schools, Conant's (1945) concept of "visibility" describes how this type of social complexity enhances democratic life and social equality. To the extent that an individual acts across an array of social settings, and to the extent that his talent or status varies across these settings, an overall higher level of uncertainty exists regarding his social status. Collectively, such a condition results in a low-visibility social structure. To illustrate how this can work in schools, imagine for a moment a ninth-grade student with mediocre athletic and academic ability attending a small junior high school where athletics and academics constitute the primary avenues of social status. For this student, the transition to a large high school with many more students and opportunities may hold a powerful liberating appeal.

Part of this appeal may stem from the number of available extracurricular activities, another key feature of comprehensive high schools linked to size, complexity, and social looseness. The availability of a wide range of extracurricular activities contributes to the blurring of status hierarchies and increases opportunity for attaining status. Conversely, a narrow range of activities will tend to highlight such hierarchies, particularly in small schools (Quiroz, Gonzales, & Frank, 1996). It is sometimes argued, for example, that in a small school, a higher percentage of the boys can make the football team. But it is also true that a boy's failure to make (or even try out for) the team will be more visible in a small school. "Failure" may result in some social stigma, and there may be few alternative ways to acquire distinction or status.

Besides their contribution to reducing status visibility, extracurricular activities contribute to democratic ethos in other ways. First, as Waller (1967) and Bidwell (1965) both note, they help rechannel the crosscurrents and countercurrents of student culture toward greater attachment to and identification with the school and its values. But they can also have the effect of pulling the school closer to the interests of students. Given the wider range of student interests and the larger number of students who potentially share these interests, a larger school's extracurriculum is likely to also be more fluid and spontaneous, shaped and driven as much by student norms, values, and informal organization as by formal design. A math teacher may decide to start a math club, but a chess club may evolve from a handful of students playing the game during or after school. In similar fashion, other political, vocational, or arts-oriented clubs may emerge. In short, there are multiple opportunities for students to affiliate with, participate in, and create "civic" activity, processes that are essential to adult democratic life.

The wide availability of activities for all types of students contributes to the townlike civic atmosphere of the school. New opportunities for semi-structured moral and ethical interaction are created, along with a set of institutions that enhance its embryonic social quality. For example, certain clubs such as Students Against Driving Drunk or Youth Ending Hunger help create a current of moral activity and awareness among the general school population. Sometimes these kinds of clubs emerge spontaneously. A good example of this is found at Edsel Ford High School in Dearborn, Michigan, one of the schools originally included in Conant's (1959) study of American high schools. While maintaining its comprehensive quality, Edsel Ford has experienced a dramatic demographic change over the past 40 years. Having once served a virtually all-white community, its students now represent a range of different races and ethnic backgrounds, including a large population of Arabic Muslims. Dearborn is home to one of the world's largest Arabic Muslim communities outside the Middle East. Once centered in a somewhat isolated neighborhood near Ford Motor Company's Rouge Plant, this community now extends throughout the city. In response to the tensions that have accompanied this change, Edsel students recently organized a Diversity Club aimed at promoting "understanding and communication beyond a student's small peer group" (Cohn, 2000).

It seems likely, and is certainly worthy of further investigation, that this grassroots institution may have helped students and teachers weather the aftermath of September 11, 2001.

Boundary Permeability

Schools are both dependent on and influenced by local community norms and values. In fact, schools maintain their legitimacy as institutions by replicating and reinforcing the cultures of the adults and students they serve (Coleman, 1961; Dreeben, 1968; Fuller & Izu, 1986; Gordon, 1957; Hallinger & Murphy, 1986). But as Coleman and Hoffer (1987) point out, local public schools once maintained a higher degree of value consistency with their surrounding communities than is the case today. School leaders could be reasonably certain of community values and concerns and, if they acted accordingly, could be reasonably certain that parents would support their decisions. Rooted in this earlier era, Conant's vision assumed a higher level of school–community trust than may be warranted today, when parents are more likely to question disciplinary or curricular decisions they feel may adversely affect their children.

This cultural tension between the school and its environment is a long-noted problem in American school literature. Tied to this problem is the issue of student culture, which can often exert a strong, distinct, and counterproductive influence on organizational goals, even when schools and parents share a reasonable level of normative congruency. With battlelike imagery, for example, Waller (1932/1967) describes the ongoing struggle of teachers and students to establish their norms in the face of "young artisans making culture for themselves and old artisans making culture for the young" (p. 107). The power of the young artisans stems from their number, their youthful energy, and the fact that they "participate in schools as a way of life, with near-total personal involvement" (Bidwell, 1965). Later studies, however, reveal the problems that can occur when students are allowed to make culture for the old. Gordon (1957) and Coleman (1961) observed how teachers often played favorites or lowered their academic standards in response to student norms and student-ascribed social status. Years later, Sedlak and his colleagues (1986) noted a similar teacher response to indifferent, disengaged, or defiant students.

Essentially, what is being described above is the tremendous potential for informal organizational elements, if left unchecked, to reshape formal goals and threaten institutional integrity. Concrete examples of the problem are not hard to find. Recalling the case of the "lost wallet" mentioned earlier, if a substantial portion of students in a school have been raised on a "finder's keepers" principle, teachers striving to convey a sense of respect for the property of others will find themselves swimming upstream. In communities with intense support for competitive sports, it can become very difficult to hold athletes to the same code of conduct as other students. A former student of mine, a principal at a nearby high school, faced six months of legal entanglements and social intimidation after he suspended the starting quarterback for throwing a punch during a game. As a former high school teacher, I noticed that over time, many of my colleagues "stopped hearing" students' hallway use of vulgar or abusive language. Others stopped noticing cheating (one colleague told me that my students' test scores would improve if I took a little walk out in the hall during the test).

While all schools face problems like these to some degree, they are more easily addressed in certain organizational settings. Small schools, magnet schools, and private schools are probably better equipped to maintain stronger boundaries, forge agreement on core beliefs and goals, and create "value communities" that attract like-minded families. For several reasons, large comprehensive high schools are restricted in all of these areas. Community complexity and diversity create conflicting incentives for teachers and administrators and a higher level of uncertainty regarding which of these need to be most closely followed. The internal complexity and diversity of the school's curriculum and teaching staff magnify this uncertainty, and it often becomes difficult to forge a set of core beliefs beyond mere peaceful coexistence.

For larger schools, this problem of protecting the integrity of core goals and values places critical importance on teachers' ability to maintain an "extended role" (Bryk & Driscoll, 1988). Such a role calls upon teachers to engage students outside the classroom and beyond academic content so as to become viewed as caring adults. Some large high schools have moved in this direction by lengthening their morning homeroom period so as to transform it into a semistructured social period with coffee, doughnuts, and an opportunity for students and teachers to talk to each other outside the constraints of classrooms, coursework, and five-minute passing time. Other schools have incorporated regular mentoring arrangements into the regular school day (Shouse & Schneider, 1993).

At the same time, teacher engagement and caring must have a bit of a tough edge, that is, be strong enough to maintain moral and intellectual order within the school despite the erosive pressures of student culture. As the studies cited above (and others) suggest, assuming this kind of role is perhaps one of the most challenging and peculiar tasks of the teaching profession. The task is significantly impeded, however, when teachers "leave their own values at the schoolhouse door" (Grant, 1988, p. 187) or, as we are about to consider, when they attempt to "automate" the task via bureaucratic or legalistic procedures. Our discussion here suggests that teachers (especially those in larger schools) need to expand their vision of professionalism to include a stronger and more proactive moral dimension. This new vision can take shape not only in interactions with students and parents, but also in those with administrators or district policies. For example, teachers might begin to deem it "professional" to resist policies that restrict their ability and discretion to act as moral agents within the school.

Bureaucratic Legalism

A theme of this chapter has been how size, diversity, and complexity enable comprehensive high schools to offer a rich and authentic version of American democratic life. But size, diversity, and complexity can also lead to greater reliance on bureaucratic relationships, thus threatening those qualities of schooling associated with the growth of democratic spirit. Particularly troubling is the increasing trend for adults in schools to shy away from or even abandon their role as moral agents. Gerald Grant (1988) points out, for example, how beginning in the 1960s schools attempted to deal with increased social uncertainty and complexity through the use of centralized authority and legal codes of behavior. Such changes, however, have led to the erosion of teachers' authority and the school's ability to exercise discretion in matters of organizational justice. Today we see this in the form of zero-tolerance policies that require students to be suspended or expelled for innocent or marginal violations of the school's formal code of conduct. Such policies permit little or no room for particularistic approaches to student discipline and moral learning, and severely constrain the school's ability to grow any sort of meaningful moral ethos beyond mere obedience to rules and authority. Teachers and principals end up acting less like caring adults, less like educational professionals, and much more like bureaucratic middlemen.

Another recent example of how high complexity and large size have harmed moral agency in schools involves the contractual transfer in many larger districts of key supervisory "duties" (e.g., hall, cafeteria, or afterschool duty) from teachers to uniformed security officers. One administrator, for example, recently commented to me that teachers in some large schools in his district have essentially withdrawn from any substantial nonclassroom interaction with students, leaving much of that responsibility to school security personnel.

Rules have always been important in schools, of course, but traditionally teachers and administrators tended to be granted a high degree of discretion in their application. But bureaucratic rigidity has led our schools to a place where the student caught fighting back against a bully receives the same punishment as the bully; where a creative writing student submitting a story with violent content may be referred for psychological counseling; and where students are barred from mentioning religious topics or reading religious materials in class. Though such occurrences may seem "rational" within a school setting, they cut against the grain of public democratic life where self-defense is considered legitimate, where violence is a common feature of popular culture, and where political leaders frequently invoke prayer in public settings.

At the risk of coming down too heavily on this point, I will offer another example to illustrate the use of such discretion. Years ago, at the public urban high school where I once taught, the violent death of a student was not an unusual event. When a death occurred, especially if word of it began spreading in the morning, it became impossible for teachers to carry on with normal class activity. Students would be deeply affected, some would be crying, and many would look to their teachers for some comforting words. It was not uncommon for teachers to offer a moment of silence, words of religious sentiment, or even an outright prayer. On one occasion, a teacher sang a brief spiritual over the school public address system. No doubt such actions were constitutionally questionable. Many schools would have refrained from any sort of spiritual response, opting instead for a more legalistic one, perhaps the use of outside "crisis counselors." I would argue, however, that my school's reaction was highly representative of American democratic life—much more similar to what would occur in a comparable situation at a local community or even national level. I suspect that the pattern of resistance against bureaucratic and legalistic rigidity was repeated in public schools across the nation in the autumn of 2001.

SOME FINAL POINTS

In this chapter I have attempted to flesh out and extend Conant's concept of democratic spirit, to examine the ability of the comprehensive high school to promote it, and to point to potential structural and organizational impediments to its development in schools. Also emphasized here have been the less formal components of school organization, largely overlooked by Conant, that can contribute to as well as detract from student moral learning. Essentially, I am suggesting that larger, more comprehensive high schools hold the potential to deliver students an experience that is socially rich, morally eventful, relatively authentic, and (when supplemented by strong curriculum) highly suited to prepare them for American civic life. To say these things is not to say that life in such schools is trouble-free for students. There will always be some social strife, apathy, or disengagement. Conflict will arise over rules and authority relationships. Students may witness amoral or unethical conduct on the part of their peers or even their teachers. As in our larger society, however, these contribute to the robustness of social life and provide opportunities for interaction and judgment, for justice and wisdom.

This picture depends, of course, on the willingness and ability of teachers and administrators to take an active authoritative moral role that extends beyond their classroom and subject matter. The word "authoritative" is key here, intended to convey the long-standing idea that authority rests with the subordinate and that adults in schools will need to work diligently to increase students' willingness to follow and trust them. The use and expansion of authority are crucial professional tasks of teaching, ones that become exceedingly difficult when antithetical values seep into organizational culture, when teachers begin to abandon their values, or when schools turn to legalistic solutions for complex moral and ethical problems, thereby compelling teachers feel to act more like "officers of the bureaucracy" (Bidwell, 1965) than educational professionals.

It is important to reiterate that no claim is made here that smaller schools cannot deliver a rich moral and ethical experience. They are limited to some degree, however, in their ability to provide the kind of social complexity, status uncertainty, and moral robustness that are so important to American democratic life. But it is also important to repeat here that "smallness" is not well defined. A high school with 600 to 1,000 students may seem small, but is probably large enough to maintain the positive social attributes described here.

The flip side of this proposition is a bit more intriguing: is a school of 2,000 to 3,000 "small enough" to allow the preservation of normative boundaries and to allow teachers to maintain an extended moral role? The discussion offered here suggests that the answer is probably yes. Also intriguing is whether teachers' willingness or ability to do so commensurately increases with substantial reductions in the size of the student population. If we're talking about a school with upwards of 5,000 students or one serving high numbers of disaffected young people, again the answer is probably yes. But for most average-size high schools, creating a strong moral and democratic ethos is probably much more a function of the will of caring adults to begin the task today.

REFERENCES

Bidwell, C. (1965). The school as a formal organization. In J. March (Ed.), *Handbook of organizations* (pp. 972–1022). Chicago: Rand McNally

Bloom, A. (1987). *The closing of the American mind*. New York: Simon and Schuster.

Bryk, A., & Driscoll, M. (1988). *The school as community: Theoretical foundations, contextual influences, and consequences for students and teachers*. Chicago: The University of Chicago Benton Center for Curriculum and Instruction.

Cohn, L. (2000). Diversity club lets students speak out. *The Detroit News*. Retrieved February 21, 2000, from http://detnews.com/2000/schools/0002/21/02210091.htm

Coleman, J. S. (1961). *The adolescent society*. New York: Free Press.

Coleman, J. S., & Hoffer, T. (1987). *Public and private high schools: The impact of communities*. New York: Basic Books.

Commission on the Reorganization of Secondary Education. (1918). *Cardinal principles of secondary education*. Washington, D.C.: U.S. Bureau of Education, Bulletin #35.

Conant, J. (1945). Public education and the structure of American society. *Teachers College Record, 47*, 145–161.

Conant, J. (1959). *The American high school today*. New York: McGraw-Hill.

Conant, J. (1964). *Shaping educational policy*. New York: McGraw-Hill.

Dewey, John. (1975). *Moral principles in education*. Carbondale, IL: Southern Illinois University Press. (Original work published in 1909)

Dreeben, R. (1968). *On what is learned in school*. Reading, MA: Addison-Wesley.

Fuller, B., & Izu, J. (1986). Explaining social cohesion: What shapes the organizational beliefs of teachers? *American Journal of Education, 94*, 501–535.

Gordon, C. (1957). *The social system of the high school*. Glencoe, IL: The Free Press.

Grant, G. (1988). *The world we created at Hamilton High*. Cambridge, MA: Harvard University Press.

Hallinger, P., & Murphy, J. (1986). The social context of effective schools. *American Journal of Education, 94*, 328–355.

Lee, V., & Smith, J. (1995). Effects of high school restructuring and size on early gains in achievement and engagement. *Sociology of Education, 68*, 241–270.

Lightfoot, S. L. (1983). *The good high school*. New York: Basic Books.

Power, C. (1997). *Understanding the character in character education*. Paper presented at L. Nucci (Chair), Developmental Perspectives and Approaches to Character Education. Symposium conducted at the meeting of the American Educational Research Association, Chicago, March 1997.

Power, C., Higgins, A., & Kohlberg, L. (1989). *Lawrence Kohlberg's approach to moral education*. New York: Columbia University Press.

Quiroz, P., Gonzales, N., & Frank, K. (1996). Carving a niche in the high school social structure: Formal and informal constraints on participation in the extra curriculum. *Research in Sociology of Education and Socialization, 11*, 93–120.

Sedlak, M., Wheeler, C., Pullin, D., & Cusick, P. (1986). *Selling students short: Classroom bargains and academic reform in the American high school*. New York: Teachers College Press.

Shouse, R., & Schneider, B. (1993). *Pepsi school challenge final report.* Chicago: Ogburn-Stouffer Center and The University of Chicago.

Sommers, C. H. (1984). Ethics without virtue: Moral education in America. *American Scholar,* Summer 1984, 381–389.

Waller, W. (1967). *The sociology of teaching.* New York: John Wiley & Sons. (Original work published in 1932)

Wraga, W. (1999). Repudiation, reinvention, and educational reform: The comprehensive high school in historical perspective. *Educational Administration Quarterly, 35,* 292–304.

5

The Comprehensive High School, Detracking and the Persistence of Social Stratification

JEANNIE OAKES AND AMY STUART WELLS

The contradictions that run throughout James Bryant Conant's 1959 argument for the comprehensive high school are alive and well in the United States today. And nowhere are they more visible than in racially diverse comprehensive high schools where educators are struggling with detracking reforms.

Conant contended that as instruments of democracy large public high schools must bring together all of the community's adolescents to experience a core of civic education, respectful social relations, and community solidarity. By 1959, most American youth were attending high school, a spectacular increase from 50 years earlier. Conant argued that by giving students of all "walks of life" access to common, comprehensive high schools, the educational system would fulfill the American promise of equality of opportunity.

Interestingly enough, Conant's espousal of the egalitarian and community-building functions of high schools did not dampen his enthusiasm for a highly differentiated curriculum structure whereby students would be sorted among courses and programs according to their "performance, inclinations, and ambitions." He defined equal opportunity as assignment to one's proper spot within a differentiated curriculum. Thus, Conant's comprehensive high schools were only partly "common" schools. That is, they were to be, like the common schools advocated by Horace Mann more than a century earlier, common to all students in a given community. But they were also to provide, through their grouping and differentiated curricula, vastly uncommon educational experiences to different students. As we note later in this chapter, Mann also advocated some differentiation of curriculum. Still, Conant, in talking about the comprehensive high school, went far beyond Mann in advocating separate and unequal classes for different students.

In this chapter, we explore the inherent contradictions in Conant's vision of the comprehensive high school as the embodiment of the American ideal of equality of opportunity, and as the institution that, by constricting students' access to curriculum and credentials, helps sort them into very unequal occupations and life chances. We do this by juxtaposing Conant's vision with national, macrolevel data on trends in economic, social, and educational inequality as well as with our more microlevel data from a study of secondary schools that were struggling to be even more democratic and egalitarian than Conant's vision.

We note that Conant's vision, as contradictory as it is, has been refined over the last 40 years. Today large comprehensive high schools are generally organized around a theory of equal opportunity that allows for unequal access. In fact, to the extent that comprehensive high schools serving students from different backgrounds and cultures continue to exist in an otherwise niche and specialty-school market, they may well owe their very existence to remaining organized around this theory. In schools where people aspire to create more democratic and less stratified and differentiated comprehensive high schools, larger political and social forces overwhelm their efforts. Still, we argue that comprehensive high schools remain some of the last sites of struggle over the issues of equality and opportunity in a diverse and divided country.

FROM COMMON SCHOOLS TO COMPREHENSIVE HIGH SCHOOLS: CONANT'S ASSUMPTIONS

Horace Mann, perhaps the best-known leader of the crusade to create common public schools in the United States, was described by Cremin (1961) as someone who poured into his vision of universal education a boundless faith in the perfectibility of human life and institutions. According to Cremin (1961), Mann believed that once public schools were established, no evil could resist their salutary influence. Universal education was, for Mann, to be the "great equalizer" of human conditions, the "balance wheel of the social machinery," and the "creator of wealth undreamed of." Poverty was certain to disappear, and with it the age-old discord between the haves and the have-nots.

Indeed, many aspects of Mann's vision were about redistribution of educational opportunities from the children of the wealthy to all children.

> Mann's school would be common, not as a school for the common people . . . but rather a school common to all people. It would be open to all, provided by the state and the local community as part of the birthright of every child. It would be for rich and poor alike, not only free but as good as any private institution. It would be nonsectarian, receiving children of all creeds, classes and backgrounds. In the warm associations of childhood Mann saw the opportunity to kindle a spirit of amity and respect which the conflicts of adult life could never destroy. In social harmony he located the primary goal of popular education. (Cremin, 1961, pp. 9–10)

Thus, in theory, the ideal of the common school presumed commonness of two types—schools enrolling all of the community's children and providing them all with a common curriculum. Mann and other common school reformers recognized that only with a heterogeneous group of students could the unifying goals of the common school be achieved. Yet Mann also recognized the conflict between the American value of individuality and the teaching of students in groups. Thus, he counseled that "children differ in temperament, ability, and interest, and that lessons should be adapted to these differences" (Cremin, 1961, p. 10).

Clearly so much of the history of American education is about how children who were believed to have different "temperament, ability, and interest"—perceived differences that often played out along race, social class, and gender lines—were given very different educational opportunities in the public educational system (Anderson, 1988; Bowles & Gintis, 1976; Oakes, 1985). Thus, the common school, begun as a vision and transformed into a myth, was never realized. It was never realized both because of the growing stratification between schools as local "communities" became more segregated by race and class and because of the stratification that occurred within schools as diverse children were assigned to different classes and groups. Schools would not realize the redistributive potential of Mann's vision. They would not become a universal system for giving all students access to all that schools could offer. Instead, exacerbated by Conant's view of the schools that he would call comprehensive, high schools have assumed the mission of preparing students for their "rightful" (often race- and class-based) places in an unequal labor market and society.

The publication of the *Cardinal Principles of Secondary Education* (Commission on the Reorganization of Secondary Education, 1918) established academic and vocational tracking as a suitable way for high schools to accommodate the increased diversity of their students, especially in urban centers with large immigrant populations. Conant eschewed this rigid tracking system, but, rather than advocating equal access to curriculum, he argued for ability-grouped academic classes that would permit schools to match students to classes in each subject where they fit best. Thus, Conant's comprehensive high school reaffirmed both Mann's call for common schools and the *Cardinal Principles'* belief in the fairness of differentiation. However, he reworked these ideas to incorporate mid-20th-century sensibilities. His version reflected, for instance, the need for larger and more efficient educational institutions. It also reflected the growing faith in the science of measuring innate ability and the Cold War focus on individual liberty, free markets, and merit-based competition (see Hammack, 1998; Lemann, 1999).

THE COMPREHENSIVE HIGH SCHOOL: TWO FUNDAMENTAL ASSUMPTIONS

Conant's claims for what the comprehensive high school could accomplish rested on two fundamental assumptions. The first is that the American rhetoric about broad social equality (Conant points out that this rhetoric is much more pronounced here than in most other industrialized countries) actually translates into an increasingly equitable distribution of opportunities and material resources. In other words, for Conant's claims about the opportunities provided in high schools to be true, broad economic and social measures of equality and well-being would have to match some of the rhetoric. Without that, the talk of equal opportunity loses its meaning as broader social and economic forces interact with the educational system.

According to Hammack (1998), Conant (1945) had written in an earlier essay that:

> One of the highly significant ideals of the American nation has been equality of opportunity. This ideal implies on the one hand, a relatively fluid social structure changing from generation to generation, and on the other, mutual respect between different vocational and economic groups, in short, a minimum of emphasis on class distinctions. (p. 163)

Similar in tone to Mann's call for common schools to be the great equalizer, Conant saw the comprehensive high school as the "instrument" that could restore fluidity to our social and economic life. Furthermore,

Conant believed that education could inculcate the "social and political ideals necessary for the development of a free and harmonious people operating an economic system based on private ownership and the profit motive but committed to the ideals of social justice."

The potential conflict between private ownership and profit motives and the ideals of social justice apparently did not occur to Conant—or at least did not command a great deal of his attention. This is no doubt in part due to his seemingly strong belief in the meritocracy, which is the second assumption underpinning Conant's argument—namely that social science could provide truly objective measures of "merit" and "ability" to be used within the educational system to decide who gets what. The comprehensive high school would use these objective measures to ensure that it is a "fair" sorting machine, and thereby conflate the sorting process with the very heart of equal opportunity. In other words, every child deserves to be well sorted, which is the first step toward achieving one's fullest opportunities.

Resting on these two assumptions, Conant argued that comprehensive high schools would both sort and differentiate while furthering the ideal of equality of opportunity in American education. Yet both national data on economic and educational stratification and our own research on educators in racially diverse secondary schools raise serious doubts about Conant's theories of opportunity and merit.

OUR STUDY OF DETRACKING SCHOOLS

During the early 1990s, we followed six public high schools and four middle schools engaged in the increasingly rare struggles to bring people with very different understandings of the world together to learn.[1] By virtue of desegregation at some of the schools and the accident of geography and school district boundaries at others, these schools had escaped the national trend toward racial and social class isolation. With their diverse student bodies and differentiated curricula, the six senior highs provide examples of Conant's comprehensive high school at the end of the 20th century. Reformers at these six schools confronted what they saw as deep pedagogical, moral, and ethical problems in their comprehensive high schools because students of different racial and ethnic backgrounds were sitting in separate and unequal classes.

The reform impulses of the teachers uncomfortable with their own experiences at the schools we studied were bolstered by research showing that curriculum tracking has harmful effects on the achievement of low-track students and that race and class play a major role in students' track placements. Many reformers believed that their schools' practices were at odds with basic American values, and that their own communities, if given the opportunity, would eagerly abandon discriminatory practices.

The experiences of these detracking high schools, however, illuminate the enduring veracity of stratification (particularly along race and social class lines) as it reflects and serves the broader economic and social stratification in U.S. society. The struggles in these school communities reveal much about how the comprehensive high school, grounded in particular conceptions of equality of opportunity and merit, stands as a bulwark against the ideal of the common public school.

BEYOND THE RHETORIC OF EQUALITY OF OPPORTUNITY

In order for Conant's vision of the comprehensive high school to match the reality of life at the turn of the millennium, his belief in the authenticity of the equality of opportunity rhetoric would need to be supported by evidence. In looking at recent information and analyses, we found evidence to the contrary.

A National Pattern of Increasing Inequality

Despite Conant's argument about the relative fluidity of the social structure and the minimum emphasis on class distinctions, there is really no evidence that such fluidity existed or that the expansion of the comprehensive high school in the later half of this century made much of an impact. In fact, recent data suggest that in reality the United States remains the most unequal society in comparison to other industrialized countries (Gustafsson & Johansson, 1999; Kawachi & Kennedy, 2002). Furthermore, longitudinal research shows that a high degree of economic inequality—both in terms of income and wealth—relative to other industrial countries has characterized the United States since its beginnings, although the inequality has grown considerably over time.

For instance, Caplow, Bahr, Modell, and Chadwick (1991) report that comparisons of wealth inequality over the history of this country show that the share of all wealth held by the richest 1% of the population increased from one-sixth to one-third over two centuries. (Furthermore, the authors note that estimates of wealth inequality are often underestimated because, in part, wealthy people try to minimize their apparent wealth and therefore their taxes.)

In recent years, despite a booming economy in the mid-1990s, the gap between the rich and poor in terms of material well-being continued to widen. Thus, while incomes rose in 1998 for most households, the gaps between the rich and the poor, and between the rich and middle-income Americans, did not narrow even in the prosperous late 1990s (Uchitelle, 1999). According to one report, "For all the boom [in the economy], income inequality continues apace, the Government concluded, with the gap between the rich and the poor failing to narrow despite the record prosperity in the late 90s in the middle and upper social reaches" (Clines, 1999, p. A8). Even the staggering losses of wealthy Americans during the recent downturn have not worked to narrow the gap between rich and poor (Mishel, Bernstein, & Boushey, 2003).

Authors and analysts differ in their explanations of this continued inequality. For instance, some commentators argue that the increase in income inequality over the last decade, let along the last 225 years, is simply the result of "individual behavior, social organization and public policy" (DeMuth, 1998, p. 8).

Other authors argue that at the end of the 20th century capitalism has evolved into "late capitalism," which brings abrupt changes in the workforce and distribution of material resources (Best & Kellner, 1991; Harvey, 1990; Hobsbawm, 1987, 1994). One of the most profound changes, these authors argue, is the way in which technology has changed the meaning and reality of "skilled" labor, allowing for greater exploitation of workers. Thus, some argue that the explanation for ongoing inequality in our increasingly technological society is that new, global technology is often less a harbinger of progress than a tool to replace salaried workers with fixed-price machinery. For instance, Aronowitz and DiFazio (1994) proclaim that all the contradictory tendencies involved in the restructuring of global capital lead to the same conclusion for workers: "unemployment, underemployment, decreasing skilled work, and relatively lower wages" (p. 3).

Rifkin (1995) argues that in the new, more technological economy, good jobs—those in the "knowledge sector" of research, engineering, computer software, law, and banking—are small in number and require a great deal of specialized training. He writes: "It is naive to believe that large numbers of unskilled and skilled blue and white collar workers will be retrained to be physicists, computer scientists, high-level technicians, molecular biologists, business consultants, lawyers, accountants, and the like" (Rifkin, 1995, p. 36). Similarly, Rothstein (1999) writes that while managerial and professional occupations will need more workers, their numbers will be relatively small compared to the openings requiring less education, including food-counter workers and waiters and waitresses.

Increased Inequality and Schooling

Whatever the explanation for the relatively large and growing inequality in the United States, the exact relationship between this inequality and the educational system is not clear. Some would argue that the inequality exists because schools have failed to provide the poorest students with the skills and human capital to succeed in the new high-tech economy. Others would argue the opposite, that the schools have virtually nothing to prepare lower-class students for—that the economy will only employ and reward a relatively small number of good jobs in the knowledge sector.

Aronowitz and DiFazio (1994), for instance, are critical of policy proposals by national leaders in the U.S. and other Western countries to invest in "human capital" through various education and job training programs—most of which, they argue, will be highly stratified based on the wealth and status of the students' families—while providing tax incentives for corporations to invest in labor-saving technology. They argue that under these conditions, investments in educational programs will not result in significant net gains in employment and will certainly not help those students from the poorest countries and the poorest families, regardless of country.

Meanwhile, Rothstein (2000) reports that the wage premium for a college degree has "soared," meaning that in 1999, a college graduate's first job typically paid 80% more than a high school graduate's first job. In 1979, this difference or college degree "premium" was only 35%. These data, combined with the broader economic picture on the growing inequality, suggest that access to higher education will separate the small number of haves from the growing number of have-nots, and that the cost of being a have-not has more than doubled in the last 20 years.

Furthermore, there is evidence that the perceived scarcity of high-paying, so-called "knowledge-sector jobs" has resulted in a great deal of middle- and upper-middle-class anxiety, as parents become increasingly focused on helping their children get the right credentials to advance to the top of the stratified educational system and labor market. In 1989, sociologist Barbara Ehrenreich wrote a compelling analysis of social and economic anxieties plaguing the current generation of upper-middle-class Americans—anxieties she called *Fear of Falling*. Doctors, lawyers, college professors, business executives, and other privileged Americans, Ehrenreich argues, have become politically conservative because they fear that their own children may not attain, as adults, their parents' affluence. They see education as the only hope for not sliding down economically, but they also worry about spiraling college costs.

These trends have had their impact on the structure of American secondary schools. Today, amidst this heightened parental anxiety, increasing economic pressures, rapid demographic shifts, and widespread dissatisfaction with public education, high schools seek new ways to be relevant to a diverse, postindustrial democracy. The most common responses further erode the ideal of the common school and perpetuate high schools' role in social sorting.

By the time *Keeping Track* was published (Oakes, 1985), most of Conant's recommendations were in place in the nation's high schools. Rather than rigidly tracked programs, for example, we found schools with a mix of heterogeneous classes (most often in electives subjects and social studies) and several ability levels of courses in mathematics, English, and science (see also Lucas, 1999; Oakes, 1987). Over time, school policies have incorporated "choice" policies that allow parents to place their students in advanced classes even if the school advises against it (Oakes & Guiton, 1995). The rhetoric and structure of tracking, ability grouping, and curriculum differentiation have changed considerably during the past 20 years—so much so that some actually claim that the most problematic versions of these practices have been eliminated in many schools (Loveless, 1999).

Lucas (1999), however, finds that the relaxing of the rigid three-track structure of academic, general, and vocational recommended by Conant has further disadvantaged students from lower-class families. Absent intact programs that make clear their consequences for students' postsecondary opportunities and course titles suggesting that classes at different ability levels are simply modified versions of the same course, lower-income families lack the experience of middle and upper-class families to recognize and negotiate placements that provide better opportunities.

By the early 1990s, schools were also feeling the effects of the broader social and economic trends. At this juncture, the schools appeared to be caught in the middle of the two competing views of the relationship between a postindustrial society. On the one hand, they were under pressure to better educate all students for the knowledge society, based on the premise that the new economy had no room for the low-skilled worker. On the other hand, they were facing increased pressure from the parents of middle- and upper-middle-class families to get these students into the relatively few places at the top of the increasingly stratified educational, social, and economic hierarchy.

Under the first view, educators kept hearing that the escalation of credential requirements for jobs in the new economy meant that schools had to provide more and more students with a college-preparatory high school curriculum. The view now prevailing in the educational policy world was that in a postindustrial knowledge society, all workers need the learning skills, problem-solving abilities, and intellectual flexibility that we previously considered only necessary for college-educated professionals or managers. Ignoring predictions of an increasing low-wage service sector where jobs require little education, most school reform was now predicated on a well-educated workforce as central to our continued economic security in a global economy. President Clinton's recent assertion (Purdum, 1996) that two years of college must become the norm for all Americans frames this view as mainstream public policy.

Some of these school reforms have brought new and increased access to a college prep curriculum and college-going for groups of low-income students and students of color who have traditionally been overrepresented in non-college-preparatory high school tracks. Mostly, however, these changes have taken the form of eliminating the remedial track, and converting the formerly noncollege or general track into the "regular college prep" track.

At the same time, the second view of the role of education in a post-industrial society—that only a select few who will gain access to the high-paying and powerful knowledge industry jobs need a challenging curriculum—was driving a proliferation of new, more exclusive routes into the highest-status postsecondary institutions. Thus, the reconstituted "regular" college preparatory classes in many schools simply sit at the bottom of a new hierarchy of class levels that include the honors and Advanced Placement options increasingly required for access into the "best" colleges and universities.

Reflecting the push of powerful, wealthy, and well-educated parents to better position their children at the top of the new educational hierarchy, AP courses have become a standard part of the upper college-preparatory track, especially in schools in the affluent neighborhoods. Since the mid-1980s, for example, the AP program has grown dramatically in states that offer students "weighted" grades that increase their grade point averages for college admission. For example, in California in 1988, 39,040 public high school students took 56,668 exams. By 1998, these numbers had grown to 87,683 students taking 145,000 exams (Institute for Education Reform, 1999). As a consequence, participation in AP (or other weighted honors courses) has become critical for students seeking to attend the University of California's most competitive campuses at Berkeley and Los Angeles, where the average entering freshman brings with him or her a high school GPA of 4.0 or better.

However, rather than being available to all students, these courses are generally restricted to those meeting strict entrance requirements. Moreover, in California's overcrowded, multitrack year-round high schools, AP courses are often restricted to one of the school's many tracks, permitting only those students enrolled in the right "track" to participate. Finally, California schools serving poor and minority students offer few or no AP courses, whereas schools in more affluent communities offer 15, 20, or more sections (Institute for Education Reform, 1999).

Rather than equalizing educational opportunity, then, new, "up-graded" academic programs lead to more differentiation under the banner of college preparation for all students. In fact, these new layers of curriculum differentiation are leading to unequal postsecondary options and status for students of different racial and socioeconomic backgrounds.

From the Perspective of Detracking Schools

From educators and parents in the detracking schools we studied, we heard a rhetoric about equality of opportunity strongly reminiscent of Conant's more than 30 years earlier. Yet as these schools struggled to break free of curriculum differentiation, the bonds between differentiated schooling and social stratification proved too strong. For example, many of the parents and educators we interviewed talked about how the stakes for gaining access to the most prestigious universities had been raised and how such college access was more critical now than ever before, given the labor market. These heightened stakes raised the anxiety levels of powerful parents and educators who saw any effort to democratize access to the high-status curriculum as jeopardizing the chances for students who in earlier years would have had a smoother path toward a place at the top of the social structure.

This parental resistance was particularly contentious among parents who felt their school was shortchanging gifted students, or using resources "meant" for one group of students on other, "less deserving" students. This belief was especially salient among a group of white parents at Liberty High, nicknamed the "Mothers of Excellence." As one lamented,

> Liberty overlooks how very important it is to academically orient kids to get an academically stimulating education. Sometimes in Liberty it gets treated as a luxury. Oh, these kids are bright, they're going to do fine anyway. Well in reality, that's not true. A lot of these kids, if they're not stimulated, are going to fall back . . . losing these kids, losing any kids is a tragedy. And it bothers me when, somehow, the district acts like losing a bright kid is not as tragic as losing the kids at the bottom.[2]

For the most part, however, powerful parents' resistance to detracking is cloaked in extremely rational and self-interested language about the quality of education their children will receive in a tracked versus a detracked class. Yet these arguments are made even when reform-minded educators provide evidence that the curriculum and instruction in heterogeneous classes can be such that all students are challenged. For example, a counselor at Central High School noted that parents of honors students will not take time to listen to teachers or administrators about pedagogical reasons for doing away with the honors track. She said they are simply "not as concerned with the whole [school] as much as they should be." A number of educators came to believe that many anxious parents were often more concerned about their children losing their privileged positions in the school than they were about the consequences of reform for learning. This response was not limited to politically conservative parents. Some of the most anxious were highly educated liberals, including university faculty, who understood well the consequences of the stratified high school for college admission. An assistant principal at Grant High School noted, for example, that "many upper class, professional parents hold occupational positions in which they work toward equity and democracy, but expect their children to be given special treatment."

This backlash not only attempted to repress detracking, but initiated new, more intense forms of differentiation within the college preparatory track. In several of the senior high schools we studied, parents considered the AP courses, with their strict entrance requirements and test-driven curricula, as critical to making their children competitive for slots in the best colleges. This parent pressure overrides the concerns of educators at these schools who complain that the AP curriculum neither provides students with access to engaging subject matter, nor involves them in inquiry-based learning experiences that teachers often see as consistent with high standards, nor allows students to engage in rigorous intellectual work with a diverse group of classmates.

In response to normative and political pressures, all the schools—intentionally or unintentionally—left some classes "out" of the reform, ensuring that the highest-achieving students could still get some sort of "special" treatment: separate honors, advanced, AP, or Regents classes exist at all of the schools. These elite classes aided several of the schools in maintaining the delicate balance between satisfying the demands of an important parental power base and providing equitable opportunities for all students. Most of the students and families who benefited from these compromises were white.

For instance, the relatively small number of "gifted" parents in the Green Valley High School community were dissatisfied with the 9th- and 10th-grade heterogeneous English curriculum, but they tolerate the classes because separate honors classes are available in 11th and 12th grade. Grant High attempted to replace their separate ninth-grade Language Arts honors classes (part of a citywide magnet program) with heterogeneous classes that offered students an honors option within those classes. However, parents of the magnet students, most of whom had been in self-contained gifted classes since early elementary school, argued vehemently that their children would suffer without separate classes. Joining forces with a powerful AP teacher at Grant, they threatened to take both the magnet school with its advanced course offerings and its mostly white participants to a nearby high school more tolerant of a stratified curriculum. On the basis of their threatening complaints, the principal refused the department's request to eliminate separate honors classes for ninth graders.

Plainview had an active parent group that worked to preserve and expand the school's AP offerings: the PTO Executive Board, a fairly tight-knit group of almost all white parents, met monthly with the principal to serve as his sounding board. One teacher noted that there was "such great community support for tracking . . . there's absolutely no way, and the administration would never want to do this anyway, that they would ever get rid of AP."

Given the structures, the norms, and the histories of comprehensive high schools, it was, perhaps, inevitable that white middle-class parents in the detracking schools we studied would trace their worries over their daughters' and sons' increasingly scarce opportunities with "problems" they associated with racial and language-minority students in their schools, most of whom were poor. In fact, one of the most prized educational resources, in the minds of many influential white parents and school officials, was a critical core of white middle-class students that seemed necessary to sustain their images of a good school. Many educators were reluctant to alter tracking policies that provide advantages to more privileged students, even if they result in racial segregation within desegregated schools, for fear of losing their most valued constituents.

At Plainview High, a school participating in contentious court-ordered desegregation, the principal was convinced that the AP course offerings were essential to maintaining the white student population. His allegiance to the AP program was grounded in his prior experiences as an administrator at Hamilton High, a nearby suburban high school. The student population at Hamilton shifted from all-white and upper-middle-class to all-black lower-middle-class to poor in a matter of 10 years. Mere mention of Hamilton and "what happened there" served as a not-so-subtle reminder of the need to appease white parents. Consequently, Plainview's principal and many faculty felt they must encourage minority achievement within the present less rigid but still tracked system, rather than attempt to disassemble tracking altogether. This concern was voiced also at Green Valley High, where opposition to detracking was fairly mild. One district administrator told us that the high school actually lost a fair amount of disillusioned white middle-class students to private schools:

> If they don't feel that there's a program here that is giving their child every opportunity, they pull their kids out and put them in private school . . . I keep saying, "The educational opportunities are there if your child chooses to take advantage of them." I think parents . . . are saying, "All of the emphasis is on giving kids a second chance, a third chance, a fourth chance." . . . The teachers are draining themselves trying to nurture kids who come to school with nothing. The other [parents] are saying, "What's in it for my child?"

Because of these pressures, educators who were committed to change often tried to straddle the fence between pleasing powerful parents and giving low-achieving students more access by reducing the number of tracks rather than dismantling the track structure. The problem with such strategies is that they reproduce a hierarchical structure supported by a culture that values the knowledge and significant life experiences of some students more than others. Rarely did the modifications bring schoolwide changes in the racial composition of classes.

Thus, tracking, like inequality in the society at large, persisted, albeit with fewer and ostensibly "higher" tracks. Just as the booming economy of the 1990s has not managed to reduce inequality in America, neither has the push for high standards in education assured greater overall equality in terms of students' access to high-status curricula. It may well be that both the economic and educational sectors of the society are highly dependent on stratification and not equality of opportunity in both realms.

THE TRUTH ABOUT "MERITOCRACY"

Conant's claim about the compatibility of sorting and curriculum differentiation with the schools' mission as a purveyor of equal opportunity rests on fair and objective decisions about which students get which opportunities. For Conant, the promise of meritocratic schooling could be realized by sorting students into academic classes according to their academic ability. However, the assumptions underlying the definition and measurement of ability suggest that merit means little more than prior family and school advantage.

The National Quest for Meritocratic Sorting

Nicholas Lemann's *The Big Test: The Secret History of the American Meritocracy* (1999) reminds us afresh of the close intertwining of our American notions of merit with biological determinism, race, and social class. Over the first half of the 20th century, psychologists pioneering the science of mental testing sought to develop measures of human ability that, among other things, would help an emerging mass society more efficiently assess intelligence, increasingly viewed as central to modern, industrial society. By the 1930s, their work was joined by Conant, who, as president of Harvard, sought measures that could shift the selection of university students from a process of "sponsored" social mobility based on family wealth, privilege, and religion to one of "contest" mobility based on a natural aristocracy of intelligence and merit (Turner, 1960). Conant did not object to social sorting per se, but he sought a sorting process grounded in innate ability, rather than in inherited privilege.

In Conant's view, equality of opportunity required a "meritocracy"—a social system in which the race for social rewards is fair. Those who reach the finish line first must be faster and thus more meritorious runners than those who come in last. Those not winning educational advantages and elite status cannot, and never will because of their own innate deficiencies (inability to run fast). For Conant, such a system would constitute a fair and "natural" sorting process for determining who should become society's elites. However, this view not only supports the status quo of a few haves and many have-nots, it also creates a commonsense notion that differences in merit are biological. In order to justify the inequalities in society, this "ideology of biological determinism" states that humans inherit their different abilities (Lewontin, 1992, p.23). Thus, nature creates a stratified society (haves and have-nots), and makes the uneven distribution of power and privilege legitimate and "natural."

However, definitions and understandings of intelligence, like all meanings, are sensitive to the cultural contexts in which they are constructed by actors (Berger & Luckman, 1966; Thompson, 1990). In culturally diverse societies, the meanings that tend to dominate are those constructed by elite groups. Because of their political, economic, and social power, elites' culturally-based definition of intelligence becomes "common sense." Accordingly, an ideology of intelligence (Mannheim, 1936) makes the particular cultural capital—the ways of knowing of the white, wealthy, and thus most powerful—not only seen as more valuable than others (Bourdieu & Passeron, 1979), but also as a function of biologically determined ability.

From the beginning, then, efforts to develop measures of ability for use in meritocratic sorting processes were tainted by racism and classism. Accompanying their belief in intelligence as genetic, most early mental testers also adhered to racial hierarchies that placed Nordics as the intellectual superiors of those of Alpine and Mediterranean races, and far above African Americans and Indians. Many of these test developers, like their colleagues in the eugenics movement, worried that the higher birthrates of darker-skinned races would eventually diminish the intelligence of the human species as a whole. (Note that this is the same argument made by Herrnstein & Murray, 1994.) So pervasive has been this logic, it is unsurprising that Conant and his peer university presidents could easily live with the "gaps" among upper-class, white Americans and applicants of lower social strata and of color on the new college admissions tests.

The belief in whites' genetic superiority has largely fallen from favor, and grouping explicitly by race and social class has become a schooling taboo. The burden of defending such practices has simply shifted from racial superiority to competitively based notions of merit The new American elite, according to Conant and his followers, would be those with innate intelligence (detected by IQ tests) whose comprehensive high schools provided them high-ability classes that prepared them for the university and for the technical and professional positions on which a meritocratic society in the 20th century depended. Today cloaked in the aura of science, the persistent stratifying effects of testing continue to make deep, unquestioned sense to many in society. The cultural capital of white and wealthy families, masquerading as meritorious "natural" abilities, rather than as a function of social location, reaps enormous advantage. (For a more detailed explication of this issue as related to tracking and detracking, see Oakes, Wells, Jones, & Datnow, 1997.)

Merit and Stratified Schooling Opportunities

That Conant's view of fair and democratic sorting in comprehensive high schools was never achieved has been documented by a host of studies that have examined the patterns of association between students' race, social class, and track placement (see Oakes, Gamoran, & Page, 1992, for a review, as well as Lucas, 1999). In the process of institutionalizing standardized psychological testing, schools also institutionalized prevailing beliefs about race and class differences in intellectual abilities. While most current grouping practices don't rely on IQ—at least exclusively—the early practices set a pattern that continues today. Standardized achievement tests, strikingly similar to IQ tests, play an important role in dividing students into ability groups and qualifying students for compensatory education programs; standardized language proficiency tests determine which class "level" is appropriate for limited-English students. IQ in conjunction with other measures remains central in the identification of gifted and cognitively disabled students. Given the context from which these merit-based practices arose, it is not surprising that students in academic tracks are disproportionately whiter and wealthier than those in other tracks. African Americans and Latinos occupy far more than their share of seats in low-track classes. Testing has consistently supported the view that low-income students and students of color have lower academic ability, and tracking practices, grounded on the ideology of testing, have created schooling conditions that fulfill those expectations (Oakes, et al., 1992).

However, developments in cognitive and developmental psychology during the past two decades have led educators and researchers to scrutinize beliefs and practices about students' intellectual capacity that had seemed rational and democratic for nearly a hundred years. Increasingly, for example, researchers have come to understand intellectual capacity as developmental and multidimensional, and learning as an active process of constructing meaning, rather than a passive event of receiving information (see, for example, Sternberg, 1986). This new view argued, from a growing base of theory and empirical evidence, that all children could be far "smarter" than conventional definitions and measures of intelligence seem to allow. The concept of genius, "superior ability," or giftedness has also shifted considerably with these new perspectives on intelligence. For example, Sternberg and Davidson (1986) claim that "giftedness is something we invent, not something we discover" (p. 4). This new work also views learning as unlimited, as opposed to the view that individuals' predetermined capacity—based on the testing of isolated skills—caps the extent of their development.

These new views of intelligence as plastic and multidimensional have gained considerable public visibility and professional acceptance. They cast fundamental doubt on the rationale for tracking structures that rigidly compartmentalize students into separate classes for "slow" and "bright" students. In response to these new conceptions, school reformers across the country, touting that "all kids can learn," have adopted an unabashedly optimistic view that schools can and must be places where *all* children, not just a few, can master rigorous academic work. The "all kids can learn" rhetoric together with the "standards" movement have suggested both an easing of the impulse to differentiate and changing definitions of merit. Across the country, Howard Garner's work on multiple intelligences has been translated into professional development programs for teachers focused on recognizing and responding to students' diverse competencies and talents (Gardner, 1983, 1988). In a number of states, recent policies have modified the procedures and measures used to identify gifted and talented students for special programs. Some even have incorporated strategies aimed explicitly at finding gifted students from low-income families and communities of color.

The rhetorical shifts make it more difficult for people to recognize that the system still works against the success of low-income and minority students. Nevertheless, most educators have only superficial knowledge of newer theories of intelligence and learning. In schools, as in the larger society, the old views of intelligence remain, as does the conflation of these views of intelligence and merit. Battles over the meaning of intelligence are often played out along race and social class lines because elite families have internalized dominant, but often unspoken, beliefs about race, culture, and intelligence. Thus, in most schools, the structural barriers to the success of large numbers of low-income students of color remain enormous. Schools' fundamental role of sorting students for lives in a socially stratified and economically disparate society remain firmly fixed, particularly in schools whose student bodies bring together diverse groups of American teenagers.

From the Perspective of Detracking Schools

At each of the schools, the conceptions of intelligence and merit that Conant embraced persisted as the skills and knowledge that educationally and economically privileged parents passed on to their children continued to be viewed as innate intelligence. These conceptions had long guided decisions about track placements and learning opportunities, and they coincided with the political context around race and class in local communities as schools attempted to detrack.

Parents of high-track students were clearly advantaged—both in educational opportunities and status—by tracking at these schools. Many exuded a strong sense of entitlement. According to these parents, their children were entitled to "more"—i.e., resources, teacher time, challenging curriculum, and better instructional strategies—because they were more intelligent and talented than other students. In this way, race consistently plays a central, if not explicit, role in the resistance of powerful elite parents to detracking reform. In a number of these racially mixed schools, white and wealthier parents feared that minority enrollment would lower educational standards as teachers tried to accommodate less able students.

Yet resistance to detracking reforms in these schools was often not primarily about curriculum or instructional strategies, but rather whose culture and style of life is valued knowledge, and thus, whose way of knowing is equated with "intelligence." Reformers soon learned that detracking was not just a structural change—although it is clearly that as well—but that it also required a profound cultural and normative shift in how they came to see students from different backgrounds.

Many educators in the schools we studied struggled mightily to use their own tenuously altered perspectives of intelligence to penetrate the fierce political opposition to detracking reforms. However, most had assimilated new meanings of intelligence in naive and incomplete renderings. Many who were eager to move away from the traditional intelligence ideology spoke clumsily about multidimensional and developmental conceptions of ability. Perhaps these ideas had been popularized by staff developers who themselves may have had only shallow understandings.

Educators at a number of schools also used new theories about the multidimensional nature of intelligence to explain and dignify racial differences in students' academic performance and school behavior. However, moving away from a reliance on traditional intelligence seems not to have diminished the tendency among many educators to judge and rank, by whatever criteria, "smart" and "not smart" children. Some teachers, for example, thought of the multiple intelligences as being distributed in much the same way as traditional IQ.

However partially understood, these new understandings did help a number of educators unravel the connections between ability tests and students' potential for learning. At some schools, educators gave greater emphasis to hard work and persistence, as opposed to conventional conceptions of ability. One Plainview teacher, for example, told us she doesn't believe in the traditional concept of intelligence. Rather, her view is that high achievement stems from a "different motivational level. A student who has more faith in his or her ability. Or more confidence. That student is going to be a higher achiever."

Educators in all of the schools attempted to extend and use the construct of the multidimensional nature of intelligence to explain and dignify racial and cultural differences in students' academic performance and school behavior. At many of the schools, explicit efforts had been made to help faculty acquire knowledge of how racial and cultural differences that are sometimes "mistaken" for low intelligence actually reflect different "learning styles." Many struggled to devise new ways for diverse students to learn productively together and to align their teaching with sociocognitive perspectives on learning. Using such techniques as Socratic Seminars, experiential curricula (e.g., project-based science and interactive math), and cooperative small-group learning, these teachers promoted instructional conversations and scaffolding in their classes. They crafted multidimensional assignments to challenge students of varying abilities. Some stressed assessments that they could justify as providing students with useful information and inclinations to work hard and successfully. Others included multicultural content to make knowledge accessible. Many found the structures, curricula, and pedagogies that are advocated for separate gifted programs to be workable practices for heterogeneous groups.

However, creating structures and school cultures that redefine who is smart and make "honors" possible for every student challenges powerful professional norms. Educators at the schools were far from unanimity on these matters. Despite some teachers' efforts to reconceptualize intelligence as multidimensional, developmental, and manifest equally across racial groups, traditional conceptions retained a firm hold. Grant's experience was quite typical. Some teachers simply held fast to a traditional view of students' abilities, and stubbornly resisted changes on that basis. But even Grant's reform-minded language arts teachers struggled with ways to judge the work of students who may be very intelligent, but who have not learned how to "jump through the hoops" traditionally expected of top students. As one teacher told us,

> Some people give me real fine indications of their intelligence, but they're not getting the grade, because the grade is the reward for the hoops. As a teacher, it would be nice to just say, "God, you're a really smart person. I'd like to give you an 'A.'" But that would then degenerate into "I like you, so I'm gonna give you an 'A.'" . . . I'm not sure, when the grading comes out, I'm not sure how I'm gonna handle this, really.

The tentativeness of these new conceptions, the widespread tendency to accommodate (or even conflate) both conventional and unconventional views, and in many cases the broad misinterpretations of newer theories of intelligence made it extraordinarily difficult for reform-minded teachers to sustain the effort and commitment needed to deconstruct more powerful ideologies of intelligence that support tracking and ability-grouping structures, particularly when parents and others used the conventional ideologies to support the racial and cultural politics in local communities.

Because the cultural biases inherent in more traditional views are strongly skewed in their favor and because the track structure is built upon those views, powerful parents generally denounced detracking reform efforts and the more recent multidimensional conceptions of intelligence upon which they are based. For example, a Plainview teacher who created a heterogenous American Studies course was asked by the principal to explain to parents the research that had persuaded her that neither society nor schools really understand intelligence or know how to measure it. Her message was not well received, particularly by those parents whose children were in Advanced Placement classes. She told us, "if you were raised under the system that said you were very intelligent and high achieving, you don't want anyone questioning that system, OK? That's just the way it is." She said that parents were most threatened by how this research was going to be used by the school, and whether it would undermine advanced classes.

As they worked to make structural and curricular changes, the reformers at these detracking high schools grappled with largely unquestioned social norms that prevented them and others from having high expectations for all students or from pressing the students toward high levels of academic competence. Each of these schools' reform efforts were jeopardized, not only by those who actively resisted reform out of concern for their children's social standing, but also by well-intentioned educators whose everyday "commonsense" actions unwittingly reconstructed the dominant culture and schooling ideologies. In the process of implementing changes in practice, they confronted mostly taken-for-granted conceptions of intelligence and ability, racial differences, and merit, and deeply entrenched traditions of what is valued curriculum and appropriate practice at the schools.

While these political battles among parents and educators were publicly fought over which kids would have access to which curriculum and which teachers, the philosophical underpinnings of these debates were far more profound. When the ideology of merit and the structure of tracking were challenged by educators who accept newer, less conventional views of ability, intelligence, and learning, powerful parents employed practices that made detracking reform politically impossible. At risk for parents of high-track and gifted-labeled students was the system of meritocracy upon which their privileged positions in society are based. As the legitimation of the schools' inequalities was challenged, it was not surprising that many grasped at any rationale to support their "commonsense" understanding of what is fair.

DETRACKING AS A RETURN TO THE COMMON SCHOOL IDEAL

As many analysts have noted, one impulse in high school reform is to turn away from large comprehensive high schools and in their place create smaller, specialized "niche" schools in the form of public magnets, charters, and other "choice" schools or support private schools with public funding. Such policies essentially abandon the comprehensive high schools' mission of providing a common site for democratic citizenship. Rather than "common" schools in which students from different backgrounds come together under one common roof, these new high school structures are more fragmented and segregated along racial and social class lines. Yet in theory they depend on common academic standards, accountability, and competition as mechanisms to ensure common expectations for students unlikely ever to occupy a common space or share experiences. At the same time, in places where high schools remain "comprehensive," the proliferation of varied academic, college-preparatory curricula has added new layers to an already highly stratified institution.

In the face of these trends, those pushing for detracking reforms worked to replace Conant's notion of the comprehensive high school with something far closer to the earlier common school ideal. For them, Conant's notion of curriculum differentiation and common socialization fell far short of democratic schooling. For example, educators at highly regarded Liberty High chafed at the realization that for all its National Merit Scholars and graduates at elite universities, the school's record of failure with low-income students of color was equally impressive. As Liberty's principal put it, "If you're in the 'haves' group, it's one of the best places in America to go to high school. If you're in the 'have nots,' it's like a lot of places—it's full of failure." Grant's reform was also was driven by a concern for equity. As one teacher told us,

> We can't afford to waste anybody. We just can't afford to say that
> we have this group of kids [the high achievers] that will carry us.
> You know, they'll be our leaders . . . I'm convinced we don't live in
> a world like that anymore. We can't afford to lose those kids.

These reformers turned to recent research in cognitive psychology and to the popular rhetoric that "all kids can learn" spawned by that research. That work, along with the movement for multicultural curricula, pressed them to not only provide all kids with access to the elite academic, college preparatory courses, but also to alter the nature of those courses to better accommodate multiple intelligences and cultural diversity. Some reinterpreted the common school to mean that, ideally, students in these schools should learn to examine the world from different cultural and political standpoints and to appreciate other perspectives, and to realize that their way of knowing the world is not the only view that matters and that knowledge is more than scoring well on a standardized test.

Surprisingly enough, at a structural level, the high schools we studied all must be judged to have been successful in very real ways. All of the schools reduced some and many eliminated all basic or remedial courses offered at their school, and some developed a common curriculum for all students in key academic subjects at some grade levels. For example, Liberty High's entire ninth-grade class was enrolled in heterogeneous two-hour English/history "cores" taught by partnered teachers, and many ninth-grade college prep math classes were heterogeneous. Students who would have traditionally been placed in a low-track English class because of low scores on the state's reading and writing proficiency exam were assigned to an English "backup" class designed to support learning in the core English classes.

Other schools provided all students with access to the schools' most challenging or "honors" curriculum. For example, Green Valley High offered challenge projects within its heterogeneously grouped English I and II classes. Students must complete at least one challenge class per quarter in order to receive an "A" in the class; simply maintaining an "A" in the regular curriculum would not suffice. Grant High's honors-option Language Arts classes allowed any student who wished to do the honors work to receive an honors designation on his or her transcript. Plainview started a campaign in which students—particularly African-American students—are pressed to attempt AP classes.

All of the schools became far more attentive to providing greater curricular access and richer learning opportunities to low-income and students of color. In some instances we found that detracking actually convinced educators in the schools we studied that low-track students are far more capable of engaging with higher-level curriculum and instruction in heterogeneous groups than they had previously thought possible. Some of the schools have even made headway in bringing together minority and white communities harmoniously under their school's roof. However, none of the reformers, as committed and skillful as they were, has achieved nearly the extent of reform that they sought, and several worry that old patterns of inequality are being replicated within their schools' new, reformed structures.

Because the changes they sought were redistributive—i.e., fundamentally altering how the schools allocated their most precious resources, including time, teachers, materials, and high-achieving students—the reformers we studied challenged traditional ways of thinking about opportunity, merit, and which students "deserve" the best that schools have to offer. Doing so, these educators became enmeshed with racial and cultural politics in local communities and the larger society. By tackling detracking reform, each of the schools became entangled in larger cultural struggle (and ambivalence) over the meaning of equality and opportunity in racially mixed settings.

CONCLUSION

The myth of Conant's comprehensive high school is that it is a place where students of all racial, class, and cultural backgrounds come together to share fair, meritocratic, and equal opportunities for success in the educational system and thus life beyond. Troubled by what they saw as the failure of their schools to provide either effective and fair curricular differentiation or a common socialization for democracy, educators at these schools engaged in a struggle to create successful schooling experiences and outcomes for all of their students. What they sought was not the realization of Conant's comprehensive high school, but rather a reassertion of the goals of the common school. They seized opportunities provided by the current school reform climate to seek new ways to knit together disparate student bodies in public schools. Their actions illuminate the resistance of educators, students, and parents to political, economic, and cultural forces to maintain a highly stratified system of educational opportunity between the classrooms; they also show why their struggles are worthwhile even if they do not achieve the broader societal results we would like to see.

The reformers we studied saw the stratified curriculum structure of their schools to be irreconcilable with equality of opportunity or a school culture aimed at fostering respectful and democratic relations among diverse groups of Americans. Ironically, their efforts to reassert the ideals of the common school as common education as well as a shared school culture seem to have strengthened as much as challenged Conant's vision of comprehensive secondary schooling. Their actions exacerbated powerful community members' unease with diverse public high schools' ability to provide high-quality academic education, and drove some families to other schooling options while provoking some educators to create new levels of stratification. This is not to say that our data suggest that stratified structures are reproduced and perpetuated in an easy or mechanical fashion. Educators, students, and parents, acting alone or together, labor mightily against the broader political, economic, and cultural forces of stratification, and at times they alter it or change its course.

By studying this process in the context of schools—the battlegrounds for these larger societal issues of opportunity and meritocracy—we see just how enduring stratification is and can be and how politically powerful the forces are that maintain it, even as it can take on a slightly different hue. Yet we also see hope and the struggle to create democratic moments and places in the face of these inexorable structures and pressures.

NOTES

1. Our interdisciplinary research team, supported in part by a grant from the Lilly Endowment, used qualitative methods to examine changes in school organization, grouping practices, and classroom pedagogy—what we call the technical aspects of these reforms—in 10 schools. We also investigated how the schools tackle well-established school and community norms and political practices that legitimize and support tracking as a "commonsense" approach to educating students. The 10 schools in the study varied in size from more than 3,000 to less then 500 students. Geographically, they were widely dispersed across the United States, with one in the Northeast, three in the Midwest, one in the South, two in the Northwest, and three in various regions of California. Different schools included significant mixes of white, African-American, Latino, Native American/Alaska Native, and/or Asian students. We visited each of these 10 schools three times between 1991 and 1993. Data collection during our site visits consisted of in-depth, semistructured tape-recorded interviews with administrators, teachers, students, parents, and community leaders, including school board members. We also observed classrooms and faculty, PTA, and school board meetings. We reviewed documents and took field

notes about our observations within the schools and the communities. Data have been compiled in extensive single-case studies that form the basis of cross-case analyses. For a full description of this study and its methodology, see Oakes & Wells, 1995. Comprehensive reports of the study's findings have been reported in papers presented at the annual meetings of the AERA and the ASA. See, for example, Oakes, Ray, and Hirshberg (1995).

2.   The quotations presented throughout this chapter capture and illustrate themes throughout the data from the schools. For each category, many more statements underlie our confidence in asserting that what is presented here represents a theme across the schools.

REFERENCES

Anderson, J. D. (1988). *The education of blacks in the south, 1860–1935*. Chapel Hill, NC: The University of North Carolina.

Aronowitz, S., & DiFazio, W. (1994). *The jobless future: Sci-tech and the dogma of work*. Minneapolis: University of Minnesota.

Berger, P. L., & Luckman, T. (1966). *The social construction of reality: A treatise in the sociology of knowledge*. New York: Doubleday.

Best, S., & Kellner, D. (1991). In search of the postmodern. In S. Best & D. Kellner (Eds.), *Postmodern theory: Critical interrogations* (pp. 1–33). New York: Guilford Press.

Bourdieu, P., & Passeron, J. (1979). *The inheritors: French students and their relation to culture* (R. Nice, Trans.). Chicago: University of Chicago.

Bowles, S., & Gintis, H. (1976). *Schooling in capitalist America*. New York: Basic Books.

Caplow, T., Bahr, H. M., Modell, J., & Chadwick, B. A. (1991). *Recent social trends in the United States 1960–1990*. Montreal: McGill-Queen's University Press.

Clines, F. X. (1999, October 2). In "boom," more lint lines pockets of poor. *The New York Times*, p. A8.

Commission on the Reorganization of Secondary Education. (1918). *Cardinal principles of secondary education*. Washington, D.C.: U.S. Bureau of Education.

Conant, J. B. (1945). Public education and the structure of American society. II. *Teachers College Record, 47*(3), 162–178.

Conant, J. B. (1959). *The American high school today: A first report to interested citizens*. New York: McGraw-Hill.

Cremin, L. (1961). *The transformation of the school: Progressivism in American education*. New York: Knopf.

DeMuth, C. C. (1998, January). Income and welfare: The new wealthy system. *Current*, p. 8

Ehrenreich, B. (1989). *Fear of falling: The inner life of the middle class*. New York: Pantheon Books.

Gardner, H. (1983). *Frames of mind: The theory of multiple intelligences*. New York: Basic Books.

Gardner, H. (1988). *The mind's new science*. New York: Basic Books.

Gustafsson, B., & Johansson, M. (1999). In search of smoking guns: What makes income inequality vary over time in different countries? *American Sociological Review, 64*, 585–605.

Hammack, F. (1998). *Seminar on the future of the comprehensive high school: A memorandum for discussion*. New York: New York University.

Harvey, D. (1990). *The condition of postmodernity*. Cambridge, MA: Blackwell.

Herrnstein, R. J., & Murray, C. (1994). *The bell curve: Intelligence and the class structure in American life*. New York: Free Press.

Hobsbawm, E. (1987). *The age of empire 1870–1914*. New York: Pantheon Books.

Hobsbawm, E. (1994). *The age of extremes, 1914–1991*. New York: Vintage Books.

Institute for Education Reform. (1999). *The Advanced Placement program: California's 1997–98 experience*. Sacramento: California State University.

Kawachi, I., & Kennedy. B. (2002). *The health of nations: Why inequality is harmful to your health*. New York: The New Press.

Lemann, N. (1999). *The big test: The secret history of the American meritocracy*. New York: Farrar, Straus, and Giroux.

Lewontin, R. C. (1992). *Biology as ideology: The doctrine of DNA*. New York: HarperPerennial.

Loveless, T. (1999). *The tracking wars*. Washington: Brookings.

Lucas, S. (1999). *Tracking inequality: Stratification and mobility in American high schools*. New York: Teachers College Press.

Mannheim, K. (1936). *Ideology and utopia*. New York: Harcourt Brace.

Mishel, L., Bernstein, J., & Boushey, H. (2003). *The state of working America, 2002–2003*. New York: Economic Policy Institute.

Oakes, J. (1985). *Keeping track: How schools structure inequality*. New Haven: Yale University Press.

Oakes, J. (1987). Tracking in secondary schools: A contextual perspective. *Educational Psychologist, 22*(2), 129–153.

Oakes, J., Gamoran, A., & Page, R. (1992). Curriculum differentiation: Opportunities, consequences, and meanings. In P. W. Jackson (Ed.), *Handbook of research on curriculum* (pp. 570–608). New York: Macmillan.

Oakes, J., & Guiton, G. (1995). Matchmaking: The dynamics of high school tracking decisions. *American Educational Research Journal, 32*(1), 3–33.

Oakes, J., Ray, K., & Hirshberg, D. (1995). *Access, press, and distributive justice: Technical, normative, and political dimensions of detracking in racially mixed secondary schools*. Paper presented at the annual meeting of the American Educational Research Association, San Francisco.

Oakes, J., & Wells, A.S. (1995). Understanding the meaning of detracking in racially mixed schools: Overview of study methods and conceptual framework. Paper presented at the Annual Meeting of the American Educational Research Association, San Francisco.

Oakes, J., Wells, A. S., Jones, M., & Datnow, A. (1997). Detracking: The social construction of ability, cultural politics, and resistance to reform. *Teachers College Record, 98*(3), 482–510.

Purdum, T. S. (1996, June 4). Clinton proposes U.S. tax credits for college aid. *New York Times*, A1.

Rifkin, J. (1995). *The end of work: The decline of the global labor force and the dawn of the post-market era.* New York: G. P. Putnam's Sons.

Rothstein, R. (1999, October 27). Shortage of skills? A high-tech myth. *The New York Times*, p. B9.

Rothstein, R. (2000, November 1). Supply, demand, wages and myth. *The New York Times*, p. B15.

Sternberg, R. J. (1986). *Applied intelligence.* Boston: Harcourt, Brace, and Janovich.

Sternberg, R. J., & Davidson, J. E. (1986). Conceptions of giftedness: A map of the terrain. In R. J. Sternberrg & J. E. Davidson (Eds.), *Conceptions of giftedness* (pp. 3–18). Cambridge: Cambridge University Press.

Thompson, J. B. (1990). *Ideology and modern culture.* Stanford, CA: Stanford University Press.

Turner, R. (1960). Sponsored and contest mobility and the school system. *American Sociological Review, 25,* 855–867.

Uchitelle, L. (1999, October 1). Rising incomes lift 1.1 million out of poverty. *The New York Times*, p. A20.

6

The Sense of Place
and Conant's Legacy
Connecting Schools and Their Communities

Mary Erina Driscoll

Schools have always played two roles in American society. On the one hand, they are linked to the familiar places of home, family, and community; on the other, they stand as the primary institution charged with preparing children for the broader worlds of polity, society, and nation. Much of James Bryant Conant's *The American High School Today* (1959) is focused on this second purpose, and his plan for the comprehensive high school, connected to the creation of a national agenda for education, held in some disfavor the benefits of localized educational perspectives. Today reformers argue anew for the merits of smaller institutions that are closely related to local and community priorities, and even amidst a powerful national agenda that moves toward standardization, the creation of such alternatives sustains the interests of many different constituencies (Raywid, 1997).

In this chapter, I will discuss the creation of the comprehensive high school as Conant's response to the American dialectic of public education. Since a sense of place animates many of the reforms that have been developed in response to the comprehensive high school, in the second part of this chapter I will articulate some central concepts of a sense of place and discuss its usefulness for understanding public education. Finally, I will return to some of Conant's central themes, considered in light of this literature.

THE AMERICAN DIALECTIC IN PUBLIC EDUCATION

The central dilemma of American education is adroitly rendered by William Proefriedt in an article published 20 years ago, "Education and Moral Purpose: The Dream Recovered." Proefriedt (1985) focuses on the role American schools played in the 20th century in beginning to achieve the dream of success and the promise of equality of opportunity. That dream, he noted, "has usually been located in the future and in the wide world out there, and yet at the same time we have seen the importance of the small town, of the local community, on one's childhood, one's past, to the fulfillment of the dream" (p. 406). Schools mirror this duality in that they are asked to play what he terms two "often conflicting" functions, i.e., to "transmit the values of the immediate society, the local or ethnic group" while at the same time they are asked to introduce the children to the broader array of values and skills that "will enable them to gain entrance to the wider world, to make their way into the future, to fulfill the dream" (pp. 406–407).

Proefriedt argues that "no author has explored the American dialectic of the home place and the wider world at greater length and with more insight" than Thomas Wolfe, and thus he invokes Wolfe's image of the train to capture this inherent ambiguity of public schools. We board the train to escape the "meanness and parochialism" of the small town, even as we mourn leaving its "innocence and salvation"; we begin a passage toward "an unexpected brighter tomorrow," even though the city of promise may be a "place of shallowness and suffering" (p. 407; see also Wolfe, 1934/68, p. 49.) Like the train itself, "The school stands between these two ambiguous points on the American cultural landscape, the small community as both supportive and constrictive, and the city, the future as both promise and peril" (Proefriedt, 1985, p. 407).

Writing near the midpoint of the century, James Bryant Conant was also occupied with this tension between the local and the cosmopolitan purposes of schooling. He understood the value and influence of the local traditions on our institutions, the ways in which our "pioneer history," the parish autonomy of the South, and the independence of New England congregations all shaped "the doctrine of local responsibility and community" that formed the political structure of our educational system (Conant, 1959, p. 9; see also Chapter 1, this volume). He also clearly saw the limits of local communities as the dominant support for American schools. He believed that schools, charged with the responsibilities of preparing individuals of varying abilities for life destinations, often faced this daunting task constrained by the limited resources available in many communities. This problem was particularly worrying in rural communities where the schools served as the most critical and often the only institution for preparing students to take on broader roles in the larger society. For Conant (1959), this tension of the American dialectic was sharpened by his belief that the destinations of all students were not the same. He was troubled in particular by those situations in which "the minority who are academically able" (pp. 15–16) might not be able to have access to the kind of curriculum that would permit them to advance to the postsecondary education for which they were suited. But he was also concerned that schools have the capacity to fulfill their duties to *every* child. As he posed it:

> Stating it another way, one can raise the question whether, under one roof and under the same management, it is possible for a school to fulfill satisfactorily three functions: Can a school at one and the same time provide a good general education for *all* the pupils as future citizens of a democracy, provide elective programs for the majority to develop useful skills, and educate adequately those with a talent for handling advanced academic subjects—particularly foreign languages and advanced mathematics? (pp. 14–15)

One of the most significant hallmarks of this concern was Conant's efforts to eliminate the very smallest schools—those with a graduating class of 100 or less—which he believed were "not in the position to provide a satisfactory education for any group of their students—the academically talented, the vocationally oriented, or the slow reader" (p. 77). The curriculum was neither "sufficiently broad nor sufficiently challenging" in such schools, he determined; moreover, given the shortage of teachers, administrators, and specialists, these schools used their staff's time "uneconomically" (p. 77). Larger high schools were required to accomplish these tasks. This push toward larger and more comprehensive schools, even at the expense of strong connections with their communities, is undoubtedly part of the legacy of this seminal report, and in the rapid expansion of school-building that accompanied the baby boomers' entry into the public school system in the years following, this recommendation had a profound influence on the kind and size of schools that were constructed.

Some four decades later there are elements of Conant's argument that remain jarring to our sensibilities, among them the harsh admission that only a minority of students were destined for further academic pursuits. But it would be unfair to Conant not to situate this concern in the national climate that produced *The American High School Today*. The final report was written only five years after the landmark civil rights decision by a Supreme Court determined to overturn local preferences for segregated schools that limited life chances for children of color. It was published at the height of post-*Sputnik* fervor that energized the educational community with national visions of bolstered defense in the face of international peril (a theme adroitly recaptured in the Reagan administration's *A Nation At Risk* [National Commission on Excellence in Education, 1983] a quarter-century later). Conant's belief that the most able of students required special consideration to connect them with the best academic resources society has to offer is shared with early architects of public schooling such as Thomas Jefferson. Indeed, Jefferson's plan for the "Diffusion of Knowledge" prescribed in detail the means through which the best and brightest of the local communities should be identified and promoted toward greater opportunities.

Another aspect of Conant's comprehensive school continues to have enormous salience for American public education. To return to our earlier metaphor, Conant's comprehensive high school is a special and complicated kind of train, one that must carry all passengers despite the fact that they are destined for multiple societal locations. The school becomes the place where individuals bound for quite different destinations can rub up against one another for at least some portion of their journey. The democratic challenge for the school is not to change these destinations, but rather to ensure that all students are socialized and equipped with the abilities and dispositions required of future citizens charged with protecting and defending the democratic faith. The school becomes the public space and laboratory for democracy emblematic of the societal values common to all.

A SENSE OF PLACE AND EDUCATIONAL REFORM

Conant's legacy is not merely the comprehensive high school, but also a kind of rhetoric that endorses the development of central educational structures in order to broaden and enlarge the educational preferences and practices of localized communities. The vestiges of that legacy can be traced to contemporary policy narratives that promote universal standards for educational curriculum and assessment, once again in order to ensure that no children are left behind by the limits of their local communities.

Over the past decades, a theme has developed in counterpoint to these positions—first to the comprehensive high school itself, and more recently to the drumbeat of national standards that aims to reduce the variance among schools and what they teach. Many education reformers are revisiting the very organizational form that Conant celebrated 40 years ago, and finding it wanting. For example, in a special issue of the *Educational Administration Quarterly* entitled "What Will Replace the Comprehensive High School," Mary Anne Raywid (1997) notes that there has been no shortage of critique for this institution, providing a litany of some of the alternatives that are currently working to supplant it. Among the "innovative and successful" schools she notes are models that emphasize connections to postsecondary education, to business and the world of work, and to the immediate environment through "expeditionary learning" as a "current manifestation of an experiential focus" (pp. 541–542).

Some of these models embody a rediscovery of the importance of a sense of place, rooting their reforms not only in a national agenda but also in a commitment to understanding the worlds in which high schools and their students are located. I do not mean to romanticize the sense of place: recall Wolfe's observation that the small town could be petty and mean as well as a source of respite and sustenance. But I believe we have neglected the importance of these local meanings too long, have "overcorrected" as we worked to address the pressing social challenges that have faced us in the 20th century. It is to this rediscovery of a sense of place, and its potential importance to education, that I turn now.

The Central Dimensions of a Sense of Place

Scholars from many different fields have examined "place" as a construct and attempted to articulate what is meant by a sense of place. Tony Hiss's (1990) summary of this movement notes that

> a brand-new science of place, growing up out of a body of formal research. . . . is examining housing projects, train stations, hospitals, and sealed and sometimes "sick" office buildings; parks, lawns and traffic-clogged streets; entrances, steps, and views from windows; meadows, fields, and forests; light, colors, noises, and scents; the horizon; small-air ions, and wind speed; and privacy. (pp. xv–xvi)

Among the individuals who share the common interest of "safeguarding, repairing and enriching our experience of place" are physicians, planners, nature writers, political scientists, management consultants, and preservationists. To this catalogue of those interested in studying place the philosopher Edward Casey (1993) would add ecologically minded geographers, remarking that "a recent undercurrent of architects, sociologists, anthropologists, ethicists and theologians, feminists, and social observers is still gathering force" (p. xv). Even a cursory examination of these perspectives gleans a rich array of meanings for "a sense of place" as well as a multitude of beliefs in its importance. Hiss (1990) states simply: "The places where we spend our time affect the people we are and can become . . . Whatever we experience in a place is both a serious environmental issue and a deeply personal one"(p. xi).

While the range and depth of this literature provide a plentiful assortment of perspectives, this multiplicity of views can also be confusing. For some, the essential elements of the construct are quite simple: "The qualities I associate with a sense of place: a lively awareness of the familiar environment, a ritual repetition, a sense of fellowship based on shared experience," writes the naturalist John Brinckerhoff Jackson (1994, p. 159). But Jackson also notes wryly that sense of place "is a much used expression, chiefly by architects but taken over by urban planners and interior decorators and the promoters of condominiums, so that it now means very little"(p. 157).

What emerges from a review of these writings is less an aggregation of concrete definitions of a sense of place and more a recurrent focus on some of its key elements. For the purposes of discussion, I will suggest four propositions for our consideration that can serve as the central dimensions of the construct of place.

Place Has a Geographic or Territorial Dimension

In many formulations, the topographic nature of place emerges as a central feature. The cultural geographers Kay Anderson and Fay Gale (1992) emphasize the territorial nature of place. They argue that

> the cultural process by which people construct their understandings of the world is an inherently geographic concern. In the course of generating new meanings and decoding existing ones, people construct spaces, places, landscapes, regions and environments. (p. 4)

Jackson (1994) notes the prevalent belief that "a sense of place comes from our response to features which are *already* there—either a beautiful natural setting or well-designed architecture" (p. 151).

For the sociologist David Hummon (1992), however, it is the interactive process *between* individual and a particular environment that is essential:

> Sense of place is inevitably dual in nature, involving both an interpretive perspective *on* the environment and an emotional reaction *to* the environment . . . Whatever the balance of emotional and cognitive components, sense of place involves a personal *orientation* toward place, in which one's understandings of place and one's feelings about place become fused in the context of environmental meaning. (p. 262)

The importance of this geographic dimension can be traced to some of the oldest formulations of the sense of place. Jackson (1994) reminds us that the term is "an awkward and ambiguous modern translation of the Latin term *genius loci,*" which referred in classical times to the "guardian divinity of that place" (p. 157). Visitors and inhabitants became aware of and paid reverence to that divinity. The phrase became associated with ritual and celebration, and "the location itself acquired a special status" (p. 157).

Thus, a geographic dimension roots a sense of place in a particular location, rendering it specific and endowed with the experiences and rituals associated with that location. As William Leach writes in *Country of Exiles* (1999), place is different from community:

> Community has been transformed into a transparent condition, barely related to concrete geographical places with histories . . . Place, of course, may contain or signify all these things—community, nature, property—in some measure, but its meaning is bound to a geographic reality both historical and profoundly lasting. (p. 7)

Places Have Boundaries

Related to the idea that place is tied to a specific geographic location is the concept that these locations have boundaries, physical and psychic coordinates that define the location. Throughout his studies, the philosopher Edward Casey (1993) repeatedly illustrates the dimensions of place by contrasting it with its opposite, "placelessness." To be placeless is to be, quite literally, adrift at sea; such a location, without boundaries and the means to orient oneself in geographic and temporal space, defies the very idea of what he means by place. To be in a place, to know it, means to limn its boundaries. Like the geographic dimension of place, this characteristic gives place a rootedness and particularity, defining what it is by also determining what it is not. As Leach (1999) writes:

> To be sure, the boundaries of place may, in the nature of things, "exclude the outsider and the stranger," as J. B. Jackson once observed in *The Necessity for Ruins*. But as Jackson also observed, boundaries "stand for law and permanence," "create neighbors," and "transform an amorphous environment into a human landscape." (pp. 179–180)

Place Is Imbued With Social and Cultural Meanings

Most of the work on place emphasizes that a sense of place is socially constructed. Places embody our culture; as Jackson notes, there may be even a ritual element to them. As Casey (1993) suggests:

For the most part, we get into places together. We partake of places in common—and reshape them in common. The culture that characterizes and shapes a given place is a shared culture, not merely superimposed upon that place but part of its very facticity. Place as we experience it is not altogether natural. If it were, it could not play the animating, decisive role it plays in our collective lives. Place, already cultural as experienced, insinuates itself into a collectivity, altering as well as constituting that collectivity. Place becomes social because it is already cultural. (p. 31)

Jackson (1994) notes that this social and cultural dimension of place is often lost in contemporary formulations. Our notions of place must extend beyond these private spaces, he argues, and be rooted in those places and structures related to groups in family and neighborhood as well as those "places and structures connected with ritual and with restricted fellowship or membership—places which we could say were extensions of the dwelling or the neighborhood: the school, the church, the lodge, the cemetery, the playing field" (p. 158).

Place Has a Temporal Quality, Linking It to Both Past and Future

Finally, many of these formulations suggest that places are interwoven with experience over time. As Casey (1993) notes, "It is by the mediation of culture that places gain historical depth"(pp. 31–2). The anthropologist Katherine Platt (1996) reminds us that this sense of history also points us toward the future. She emphasizes the generative elements of place, along with its capacity for historical imagination. "Places capture experience and store it symbolically. Its collective meanings are extractable and readable by its later inhabitants"(p. 112). This historical dimension, however, does not turn us only toward the past.

Places of experience . . . also are platforms for visions and plans about the future. Places of experience provision us with identity to venture forth out of this place into less certain or orderly spaces. Places of experience provide categories for managing new adventures and new cycles of old adventures. Places of experience connect the past to the future, memory to expectation, in an invigorating way. Places of experience give us a sense of continuity and energy. (p. 112)

I will now turn briefly to some general implications of this concept of education, many of which have been developed at greater length elsewhere (see Driscoll, 2001; Driscoll & Goldring, 2003; Driscoll & Kerchner, 1999). In the final section of this chapter, I will link the sense of place to two particular elements in Conant's work and his legacy of the comprehensive high school.

How Is a Concept of Place Useful in Understanding Schools and School Reform?

First, understanding a sense of place has the potential to generate insights, drawn from several disciplines, that may provide a useful counterpoint to our dominant assumptions about schools and school systems. The language of efficiency and standardization has long been our native tongue as we consider these institutions. The image of schools and their communities as unique places, with deep local connections and singular sets of resources, cannot help but to enrich our discourse. The development of a sense of place with particular resonance for the educational community is similar to the re-envisioning of schools as communities that has preoccupied us over the past several years. Such a metaphor can provide a powerful alternative image to the bureaucratic icons of schooling with which we have become so familiar. Place, like community, is a concept rooted in multiple ways of knowing that can offer fresh perspectives on how we think about educational institutions.

Second, the physicality or the geographic nature of place understandings can be especially helpful as we consider schools today. This is important as we face the challenge of rebuilding a system that is in many cases characterized by crumbling, outdated, and inappropriate physical facilities, too often located in crumbling communities. Our attention to school facilities and their effect on education is vital and emerges as an even more pressing need day by day. Duke (1998), in a review of the literature that connects learning opportunities with the quality of the physical environments in which that learning takes place, documents the alarming conditions of school buildings throughout the country. Uline (2000) reminds us that the quality of the spaces we construct and maintain for educational purposes matters, and our sense of the physical environment must be connected to deep understandings about the teaching and learning activities that occur there.

Third, this construct of place can draw attention to the ways in which communities and schools define overlapping boundaries. Too often the boundaries of the educational place are drawn at the four walls of the school, with the surrounding community left an uncharted land at best and a source of trouble at worst. But a sense of place invites a much broader envisioning of the landscape, one that moves away from the "fortress" mentality of many schools. Here ideas of safety and security are generated from knowing who we are, rather than from keeping strangers out. Thinking about the contexts and communities that support the school is also consonant with the kind of "asset mapping" of communities and their resources that is espoused by McKnight and Kretzmann (McKnight, 1995; Kretzmann & McKnight, 1993, 1996). In this view, the deficit models of communities that have often characterized inner-city settings is countered with a methodology that systematically draws attention to the multiplicity of resources—cultural, social, and physical—that may be found in the communities that support schools.

Fourth, a sense of place can help to provide a deep awareness of the importance of history in the social construction of neighborhoods and schools. This is not to assert that all history is inspiring, and much of it may and should be contested. Wallace Stegner (1992) has remarked that we "threw overboard" the baggage of history when we found it recalled "bloody memories" and "old tyrannies" (p. 206). But we do so at our peril, he continues, and it is only by understanding the history of our places can we fashion a healthy society and "acquire the sense not of ownership but of belonging" (p. 206).

Finally, connections to place may contribute to the development of sustained engagement that permits students to gain the kind of deep knowledge that will inform their understandings in other locations. This is what Katherine Platt means when she talks about how places of experience give us the ability to venture forth into the spaces we do not yet know. Some of those who study place argue that only by understanding and sustaining our connections with the particular worlds of our experience can we grow to a more global understanding of the world at large and its needs. As Leach (1999) argues,

> A strong sense of place, along with the boundaries that shape it and give it meaning, not only fosters creativity but also helps to provide people—especially children—with an assurance that they will be protected and not abandoned . . . It is indisputable that children need a sense of place (along with an acceptance of boundaries that define and establish the safeness of place) in order to become self-reliant. (p. 179)

In summary, the construct of place outlined above "rests on repeated activities, the social construction of shared knowledge over time, prolonged interaction with an environment, and knowledge as well of participation in the history created there" (Driscoll, 2001, p. 39). This construct enables us to expand our vocabulary, focus on physical spaces in a way that is essential, transform our ideas of the boundaries that shape both schools and communities, embrace the history that can inform the present and the future, and provide a context for specific knowledge that becomes the basis for new and expanded perspectives.

CONANT'S LEGACY AND THE SENSE OF PLACE

The comprehensive high school as Conant conceived it was an institutional response to some enduring dilemmas in American education. One of these issues was the need to devise adequate educational structures to accommodate the varying intellectual skills of the children in any community. The second required addressing the complicated role that schools must play as institutions that prepare youth for different life courses even as they are charged with inculcating the values of democratic citizenship for all. The ideas of place that animate some forms of current educational reform may provide fresh insights as we imagine what Conant's legacy might look like in the years to come.

Ways of Knowing and Learning Across a Spectrum of Individuals

Conant's assessment of the range of intellectual abilities that might be found in a given school was consonant not merely with contemporaneous conceptions of how mental abilities varied across the general population. It was also informed by the prevalent thinking about the fixed nature of intelligence itself, as well as by a belief that intellectual ability could be reliably measured in a robust fashion at any point in the life span. Informed and energized by the instruments developed by the educational scientists of the early 20th century, this belief was reified even further by the widespread use of those intelligence tests through most of the 20th century. Schools were organized in ways that reflected their acknowledgment that students fell into different categories of intellectual prowess.

The misuse of those tests and the limits in life chances that were created by such primitive intellectual categorization by schools has been well documented elsewhere (Tyack, 1974; Tyack & Hansot, 1982). Conant's assertions about the variance of ability, however, were certainly in line with what would be considered the standard educational thinking and practice of his time.

What strikes us today is not just the fixed categorization of intelligence and the rigid response to this perceived reality on the part of schools. Constructions of intelligence itself—what it is comprised of, its fluidity, and its ability to be reliably measured given standard assessments—have also shifted dramatically since Conant wrote *The American High School Today*. Howard Gardner, for example (1983), postulates intelligence not as a unitary construct but rather as a set of complex understandings that together comprise the "multiple intelligences" of the human being.

The work of cognitive psychologists in particular and their exposition of what has been termed the "new science" of learning are also significant in this respect (Bransford, Brown, & Cocking, 2000). In brief, this new science emphasizes the contextual nature of knowledge. The learner must scaffold new knowledge onto existing structures. It is through deep understanding of one context that one is able to develop the kind of generative knowledge that enables the transfer of learning to a new setting. The same tasks are required of all learners, although the construction of this relational knowledge may occur more rapidly in some learners or be affected by the level of expertise one has gained through experience. The most robust learning occurs in learning communities in which individuals form and test their conceptions of the world in concert with other learners (Bransford et al., 2000; see also Driscoll & Goldring, 2003).

Our current conception of intelligence and of the science of learning, then, leads us to a somewhat different answer to the problem with which Conant wrestled. Providing adequate experiences for all children still requires a threshold of resources to address their multiple needs. But meeting this challenge may require a deeper understanding of the place-formed cognitive structures that every child brings to the classroom than Conant envisioned. Moreover, this science encourages us to connect more fully with the contexts and communities in which children live outside of school in order to build most effectively on the knowledge they bring to the classroom and to facilitate learning across many contexts. This vision of learning, coupled with an understanding of a sense of place, yields some interesting perspectives. Such a view focuses us much less on the limits of a localized perspective and much more on the need for schools to develop textured understandings of the communities in which they are located, in order that all learners may integrate knowledge in and out of school (Honig, Kahne, & McLaughlin, 2001).

Conant's focus on how we provide adequate resources, and the need to deal with the variations we perceive across individuals, is still astute. Our response to these issues, however, should now be informed by a complicated and fluid conception of intelligence, one that respects and exploits the life experiences that students bring to their own learning (see Driscoll & Goldring, 2003, for further development of this point).

The Common Core of the Comprehensive High School

As noted earlier (see Chapter 1, this volume), Conant's comprehensive high school was built on ideas of common education for democracy. This notion of the school as a public space in which all individuals must negotiate the civil relationships required for a democratic society is perhaps the most important element of Conant's legacy. Critics of small, specialized schools have argued that such responses to comprehensiveness privilege individual choice over the common good and permit smaller segments of society to create educational spaces that may not promote basic democratic values. But schools that connect to particular places need not be intrinsically isolationist or excessively privileged in their worldview, especially if they take to heart the challenges that John Dewey (1900) articulated with such eloquence when he envisioned his version of a common school over a century ago. For Dewey (1916), the school was both connected to the place in which it was located and a microcosm of the democratic society to which students aspired. Only through the society of the school can individuals construct their understandings of democracy and what constitutes a good life. No school—large or small, comprehensive or specialized—may shirk this most critical function of American education.

Conant's concern about developing democratic schools is as prescient as ever, but our response to the challenge laid down by Dewey some 50 years before him may look somewhat different today than what either envisioned. Recapturing a sense of place in American schooling may hold the promise of constructing more deeply embedded structures for democratic practice. As Leach asserts, these connections are essential if we are to build a productive and compassionate society:

> Without a sense of boundaried place, finally, there can be no citizenship, no basis for common bonds to others, no willingness to give to the commonweal or to be taxed, even lightly, in behalf of the welfare of others . . . A living sense of a boundaried place, some kind of patriotism beyond love of abstract principles, is the main condition for citizenship . . . This living sense always has a provincial character. It takes shape first as connections to families and friends, then to neighborhoods, towns, and regions, and finally, to the nation and the world. It is through the formation of this *sense of place,* beginning with the home and parents, that people develop their *loyalty to place,* but it is only after the earliest concrete ties are formed that the bigger connections can be forged; the process cannot begin the other way around. (pp. 179–180)

A Final Caution

Wolfe's train as the vehicle that brings the young man from the small town to the big city may seem anachronistic today; his skepticism about romantic notions of small towns and communities, however, is not. In some cases Conant's ideas of providing adequate resources for all and of creating a public space for democratic learning have been realized in forms that permute the very goals he espoused. It is vital to realize that some schools that are informed and attentive to a sense of place may also run the risk of becoming xenophobic or myopic communities that do not embrace the charge of creating contexts for learning that expand the life opportunities for all children.

Neither Wolfe nor Conant nor even Dewey could have envisioned the virtual world of technology and communication available to children today to expand one's horizons. To move beyond the home and one's own lived experience requires not a train but rather a burgeoning array of electronic devices. Such limitless possibilities for connections with a global society paradoxically demand that students know their own place even more thoroughly in order to make sense of the world beyond.

The world we face today is no less perilous than the one to which Conant addressed his concerns in 1959. Schools are still the best places for children to develop that essential knowledge, rooted in a learning community that is committed to public, democratic discourse. A cautious and thoughtful reimagination of a sense of place will help as we create the next generation of schools for the 21st century.

REFERENCES

Anderson, K., & Gale, F. (1992). Introduction. In K. Anderson & F. Gale (Eds.), *Inventing places: Studies in cultural geography* (pp. 1–14). Melbourne, Australia: Longman Cheshire.

Bransford, J., Brown, A., & Cocking, R. (Eds). (2000). *How people learn: Brain, mind, experience and school.* Commission on Behavioral and Social Sciences and Education, National Research Council. Washington, D.C.: National Academy Press.

Casey, E. (1993). *Getting back into place: Toward a renewed understanding of the place-world.* Bloomington, IN: Indiana University Press.

Conant, J. B. (1959). *The American high school today.* New York: McGraw-Hill.

Dewey, J. (1900). *The school and society.* Chicago; University of Chicago Press.

Dewey, J. (1916). *Democracy and education.* New York: Macmillan.

Driscoll, M. E. (2001). The sense of place and the neighborhood school: Implications for building social capital and for community development. In R. Crowson (Ed.), *Community development and school reform* (pp. 19–41). New York: JAI Press.

Driscoll, M. E., & Goldring, E. (2003). *Schools and communities as contexts for student learning: New directions for research in educational leadership.* Paper presented at the Annual Meeting of American Educational Research Association, Chicago, IL.

Driscoll, M. E., & Kerchner, C. (1999). The implications of social capital for schools, communities and cities: Educational administration as if a sense of place mattered. In J. Murphy & K. Louis (Eds.), *Handbook of research on educational administration* (2nd ed.) (pp. 385–404). San Francisco: Jossey Bass.

Duke, D. (1998). *Does it matter where our children learn?* A Policy Perspectives Paper. Charlottesville, VA: Thomas Jefferson Center for Educational Design at the University of Virginia.

Gardner, H. (1983). *Frames of mind.* New York: Basic Books.

Hiss, T. (1990). *The experience of place.* New York: Vintage Books.

Honig, M., Kahne, J., & McLaughlin, M. (2001). School–community connections: strengthening opportunity to learn and opportunity to teach. In V. Richardson (Ed.), *Handbook of research on teaching, 4th edition* (pp. 998–1028). Washington, D.C.: American Educational Research Association.

Hummon, D. (1992). Community attachment: Local sentiment and a sense of place. In I. Altman & S. Low (Eds.), *Place attachment* (pp. 253–278). New York: Plenum Press.

Jackson, J. B. (1994). *A sense of place, a sense of time.* New Haven, CT: Yale University Press.

Kretzmann, J., & McKnight, J. (1993). *Building communities from the inside out: A path toward finding and mobilizing a community's assets.* Evanston, IL: Asset Based Community Development Institute at Northwestern University.

Kretzmann, J., & McKnight, J. (1996). Assets based community development. *National Civic Review, 85,* 23–29.

Leach, W. (1999). *Country of exiles: The destruction of place in American life.* New York: Pantheon.

McKnight, J. L. (1995). *The careless society: Community and its counterfeits.* New York: Basic Books.

National Commission on Excellence in Education. (1983). *A nation at risk.* Washington, D.C.: National Commission on Excellence in Education.

Platt, K. (1996). Places of experience and the experience of place. In L. Rouner (Ed.), *The longing for home* (pp. 112–127). Notre Dame, IN: University of Notre Dame Press.

Proefriedt, W. (1985). Education and moral purpose: The dream recovered. *Teachers College Record, 86* (3), 399–410.

Raywid, M. A. (1997). About replacing the comprehensive high school. *Educational Administration Quarterly, 33* (Supplement), 541–545.

Stegner, W. (1992). The sense of place. In W. Stegner (Ed.), *Where the bluebird sings to the lemonade springs: Living and writing in the West* (pp. 196–206). New York: Penguin Books.

Tyack, D. (1974). *The one best system.* Cambridge, MA: Harvard University Press.

Tyack, D., & Hansot, E. (1982). *Managers of virtue: Public school leadership in America, 1820–1980.* New York: Basic Books.

Uline, C. L. (2000). Decent facilities and learning: Thirman A. Milner Elementary School and beyond. *Teachers College Record,* 102(2), 442–460.

Wolfe, T. (1934/1968). *You can't go home again.* New York: Harper & Row.

7

Does the Comprehensive High School Have a Future?

FLOYD M. HAMMACK

As a number of the chapters in this collection attest, the comprehensive high school today represents a negative image, one implying an outdated organizational form that is unresponsive to our current educational needs. The key criticism is that the schools are too large and try to do too many things, none of them very well. This critique is particularly strong when aimed at urban high schools, where the organizational characteristics are viewed as having especially negative consequences for the continued academic motivation and achievement of poor and minority youth. Lacking community- and home-based resources necessary for continued academic achievement, these students too often become alienated from the school and withdraw from its moral order. Too often they leave the school altogether before graduation without the levels of academic skills required by the labor market today (Angus & Mirel, 1999).

There are many versions of this critique of comprehensive high schools, but it would do well to remind ourselves of the origins and the alternatives out of which the idea of comprehensiveness emerged. As we contemplate alternative forms of secondary school organization, it is critical to pay attention to the problems the comprehensive model of secondary education originally was designed to address. While the form or shape of these problems may change over time, I will make the argument below that, in fact, the paramount problem for the comprehensive high school remains for us unresolved.

The enduring issue of secondary education is, and has been, how to organize instruction for students of widely differing levels of primary and/ or middle school preparation, ability, interest, and career trajectories. As was detailed in Chapter 1, the expansion of enrollment through the first half of the 20th century to include most adolescents created a student body in which only a minority aspired to higher education. Arguing that the college preparatory function of the earlier secondary schools was increasingly irrelevant to many students and their parents, educators put in place curricula with more practical outcomes, especially labor market advantages. This new, comprehensive conception of the high school role was well developed in the *Cardinal Principles of Secondary Education* report (Commisson on the Reorganization of Secondary Education, 1918).

This document argued that secondary education should be available for all the youth of the community, not just the few who were college-bound. This vision offered an idea of secondary schooling in direct opposition to the *Committee of Ten Report* (National Educational Association, 1894), developed by the same organizations nearly 20 years earlier. This group thought all secondary students, whatever their ultimate adult destination, needed the mental discipline that a traditional curriculum, or a close variant, offered. Twenty years later, this theory of mental development and of secondary school curricula was rejected (but see Resnick's 1999 rehabilitation of this report).

The idea of an academic curricula for all was not accepted by the authors of the *Cardinal Principles* report. Drawing on the annual reports of Horace Mann (1976, originally 1848), this report encouraged educators to develop a variety of curricula, including vocationally oriented courses of study for those students in the community who sought more immediate rewards from their education. At the same time, the *Cardinal Principles'* authors were concerned with the consequences of the evolving society around them: for example, industrialism and urbanization were leading to a loss of social cohesion. They thought a schooling experience shared by *all* of a community's youth through early adulthood was imperative in the service of social solidarity. In one widely cited passage, they argued that the son of the factory owner should go to the same school as the future janitor in that factory.

Within a few years of the issuing of the *Report*, most of the students in comprehensive high schools were enrolled in general or vocational courses of study. A minority pursued a college preparatory curriculum. The high school had been transformed for the first time from a preparatory institution to a terminal one (Trow, 1961). Whether these schools were comprehensive in the sense that the authors of the *Cardinal Principles* report envisioned, however, is questionable. As Rury concludes in his assessment of the concept included in Chapter 3, what the promoters of comprehensive high schools had proposed met the hard realities of post–World War II demographics and mobility. Suburbanization made urban high schools far from comprehensive, at least in the sense of enrolling a cross-section of a community's youth. Suburban schools inevitably reflected the economic and social composition of their residents, and these were seldom very diverse. Some older small and midsize towns have schools that remained comprehensive in this regard, but these have become a significantly smaller proportion of U.S. high schools (Levine, 1966).

In urban areas, enrollments became increasingly poor and minority, and specialized high schools, sometimes older academic ones like Central High School in Philadelphia (Labaree, 1988), were somewhat protected from these demographic trends. Truly comprehensive high schools may have been present in urban areas, but by the post–World War II era they were rare. Most of the large urban high schools, so criticized today, have not been comprehensive in any meaningful sense, if they ever were.

The change to high schools with differentiated curricula was not uncontroversial. As Angus and Mirel (1999) discuss, defenders of a single curriculum emphasizing college preparation never gave up. Often they enlisted national defense in their arguments, stressing the lower quality of the vocational and general curricula and the lower performance of students and how this affected our nation's ability to defend itself. But the speed of the expansion of high school enrollments, especially from 1915 to 1935 (see Goldin, 1998), was unprecedented and offered a tremendous challenge to educators. They faced the necessity of offering programs of study that satisfied their new constituencies, a majority of whom were not headed to college.

As Krug (1972) and others have told the story of this process, the first half of the 20th century is one of the erosion of the college preparatory function in favor of more general and vocational curricula. There is ample reason to view the second half as the beginning of the rehabilitation of the college preparatory curriculum and its rise again to dominance. Two related factors are usually cited as stimulating this development: the precipitous decline in the economic payoff of the high school diploma and the high level of (and increasing) enrollments in postsecondary educational institutions. The growth of postsecondary enrollment, in part stimulated by the declining value of the high school diploma, has followed a pattern in the second half of the 20th century that parallels the growth of the high school during the first half (Dougherty, 1997).

Today, with so many high school graduates going on to college—in some states over 70%—anything less than a college preparatory curriculum seems to many to be absurd at best, and racist or classist at worst. To address this issue, in state after state, policymakers have instituted high school graduation exams that are built on the notion that all students should have college-preparation level skills as they leave high school. The possibility of several, quite different curricula all ending in a high school diploma, a cornerstone of the comprehensive idea, finds virtually no support today, though some do question this policy (Rosenbaum, 2001; Wilensky, 2001).

In New York, for example, the tradition of two different diplomas based on different and unequal state tests has been eliminated in favor of a single diploma based on the Regents exams that historically were only taken by students seeking college admissions. The less difficult examination, the Regents Competency Test (RCT), has been retired, and the diploma associated with it is no longer offered. Because this diploma was more common among graduates of urban and often poorer neighborhoods, it came to be identified as racist, epitomizing the lower expectations and lower performance of a segregated educational system. Such a system, once defended as responsive to the needs of all of a community's youth, is today understood by many as a last vestige of the patronizing racism of earlier periods.

Thus, today, around the country as well as in New York, the call is for a college preparatory curriculum for all students. None of the current school reform models call for comprehensive high schools. How successful these efforts will be remains to be seen. In New York City, there is concern that many of those who are supposed to graduate will have not passed the required Regents tests, even though the passing grade has been reduced. The dropout rate has increased recently, after steady declines for a number of years (Hartocollis, 2001; Rothstein, 2002). Others are concerned that there will be a surge in students opting out in favor of the GED. A substantial proportion of students take more than four years to graduate from high school. Yet advocates of a single college-level diploma stress that in our contemporary economy, without an appropriate education, students will be locked out of job opportunities. The evidence of declining opportunities and of low incomes for those with only a high school diploma is stark (National Center for Educational Statistics, 1997). Thus, the argument goes, all students need to meet the new higher standards.

It is not, however, that the high school curriculum is becoming less differentiated. As I noted in Chapter 1, there has been a large increase in the number of high schools offering Advanced Placement (AP) classes and an increasing number of subjects included in the AP program. This has resulted in an increase in the number of students taking the AP examinations that colleges can use to award college credit (Viadero, 2001). But note that the expansion of this program may be seen to have gone too far;

Harvard has recently announced that only students who received the highest score on an AP test will be eligible for advanced standing (Lewin, 2002).

So-called "dual enrollment" programs have also grown, where high school students simultaneously enroll in college-credit–bearing courses either at their home high schools or at local colleges (Boas, 2002; Gehring, 2001a). The increase in International Baccalaureate (IB) programs in secondary schools likewise testifies to the increasingly upward extension of the academic high school curriculum for some students (Gehring, 2001b).

Oakes and Wells in Chapter 5 take note of this increasing differentiation at the upper end of the secondary curriculum and see it as simply a new form of the older comprehensive school process known as tracking. They assert that the new tracking represented by layers of curriculum differentiation is producing unequal postsecondary options, especially for minority students and those from poor families. These authors think the time is ripe for a return to the idea of a common school, like the 19th-century model of Horace Mann, referred to earlier.

DOES THE COMPREHENSIVE HIGH SCHOOL IDEA HAVE ANY RELEVANCE FOR HIGH SCHOOL REFORM TODAY?

It is important to remember that the problem the comprehensive high school was created to address was how to satisfy the needs of increasingly diverse students. Today, that problem remains critical, especially in urban areas. Across the country, the high school student body is growing and is increasingly diverse. This diversity is at least as great as during the first half of the 20th century, when the comprehensive high school came into existence. Thus, the question of how to best organize students for purposes of instruction is as significant today as it was at the turn of the last century.

While some propose greater use of cooperative learning and other new pedagogical strategies appropriate for heterogeneous grouping, such as Oakes and Wells suggest in Chapter 5, others propose smaller schools and smaller classes so as to limit student variability and its consequences (Rubenstein, 2001). Other models also try to limit student variability, such as through the creation of smaller schools-within-schools based on career academies whose students share a common interest (see Legters, Balfanz, Jordan, & McPartland, 2002). Schools of choice, however configured, concentrate students with similar perspectives, outlooks, and aspirations. The breadth of students being educated under one roof, which was addressed in comprehensive high schools through internal curriculum differentiation, is not addressed in most current high school reform models (Kahlenberg, 2001).

The effort to bring all students to a college-prep level of achievement is motivated out of a desire to enable all students to benefit from the opportunities available only to those who attend college and, increasingly, those who graduate from college. This single mission for the high school emphasizes the academic function of the secondary school, and seeks to maximize the individual payoff of educational achievement, as discussed by McDonald in Chapter 2. The social integration mission, so clearly articulated by the *Cardinal Principles* report and endorsed by Conant, is seldom mentioned today. It seems as though we have to choose between the best way to afford more equal individual benefits at the expense of benefits that are communal. Of course, the community benefits from the taxes and other contributions of those higher up on the economic ladder, but the social solidarity that may be afforded through more comprehensive schools, especially more racially integrated schools (as Orfield & Gordon, 2001, point out), is significant.

This book has not examined all the reform models that are competing for prominence among policymakers and educators today, but this is a good place to identify some of their common elements and relate them to the idea of comprehensiveness that informed earlier ideas about secondary education in the United States. Common among many of the reform models is a single or core curriculum, often aligned with new state standards and assessment tools. The content of these core courses can vary somewhat in rigor or level of work demanded of students, but all models challenge educators not to "water down" content so that students are denied equal opportunities to learn (Gamoran, Porter, Smithson, & White, 1997). The existence of exit tests, such as the Regents examinations in New York, are frequently cited as a positive means of focusing the attention and motivation of students.

Barriers to the successful implementation of such a core curriculum have been identified by Oakes (1992) in their research on detracking. The most important one they identify is a technical one—how to provide high-level instruction to heterogeneously grouped classrooms. Even the most successful attempts at requiring college-preparatory math classes, for example, while increasing the proportion of low-achieving students who take and pass such courses, nevertheless leaves "substantial numbers of disadvantaged students [who] still fail their math courses" (Gamoran, 2000, p. 111). The "technical" problems involving curriculum and instruction are real, and addressing them will go some distance in reducing other barriers (normative and political ones, for example; see Cohen & Lotan, 1997; Oakes, 1992). The attempt to provide a college-preparatory education for all our youth is without precedent, but then so too was our effort to provide a secondary education, however differentiated, to all our youth in an earlier era.

The core course idea would provide for the possibility of the school addressing the social integration function, or the "democratic spirit" idea mentioned by Conant (and as I noted earlier, the *Cardinal Principles* report and Horace Mann). As Roger Shouse notes in Chapter 4, this "spirit" was thought to result from bringing together students from across the spectrum of a community. Not only does the core-course high school propose to offer equal learning opportunities, at least in theory, it could also offer the possibility of providing the curriculum to a cross section of the community's youth.

Another common element in a number of reform models calls for the integration of work-oriented learning with an academic curriculum. The High Schools That Work model (Bottoms, Presson, & Johnson, 1992) and various forms of career academy schools-within-a-school models (such as the Talent Development High School described in Legters et al., 2002) illustrate these common elements. While offering students choice of career-relatedness in their courses, the effort is not to allow curriculum differentiation by academic level or rigor, but only according to career field relevance.

As with all schools-within-a-school or free standing small schools with a special curricular focus, the concern is that the enrollments in these schools truly reflect a cross-section of the community's youth. A good example of this concern is the cautionary note in Croninger, Johnson, and Bodone (2000; also see Ready, Lee, & LoGerfo, 2000), who closely studied several schools that been broken up into schools-within-a-school. They found strong pressures to raise achievement levels and demonstrate improvement in all of the schools they studied. At each of these schools, they saw evidence of administrators and individual subunits using selective admissions practices and implementing a tracked curriculum.

As with charter schools that use various forms of requirements for admissions (e.g., Cobb & Glass, 1999), the possibilities of some students being "creamed" off to attend schools deemed better in some respect than others is ever-present (Lee, Croninger, & Smith, 1996). With parents viewing schooling as increasingly important to their children's future, competition among them for the "choice" schools can be extreme. For example, recently some New York parents, hoping to enroll their five-year-old children in what is perceived as a "good" school, waited in line for more than two days. This is a common event around the country and clearly demonstrates the sacrifices many parents are willing to make to obtain a favorable educational advantage for their children.

Such a commitment on the part of parents, however, may reinforce existing inequalities. As discussed by Oakes and Wells in Chapter 5, Lucas (1999) noted how important information has become as educational options and choices proliferate. He focused on secondary schools, and examined how high schools have moved away from tightly structured curriculum tracks. Students today have many more choices for courses, not all of which are as useful for meeting college entry requirements. "Ironically, the dismantling of formal [tracking] programs has probably *increased* the information gap between haves and have-nots" (p. 132).

The parental information gap is one likely source of the achievement gap. As small schools proliferate and the number of charter schools increases, the idea that schools at the same level offer an equivalent education becomes obsolete. Schools are different by design (Metz, 2003), and the consequences of where students go to high school are significant. Of course, where one went to school has always been important (there is a reason why much information about schools is located in the real estate section of the local papers), but as schools become more differentiated from each other—and not as internally differentiated as strict tracking previously provided—information about schools and about courses looms even more crucial. Ironically, these parental efforts can sometimes backfire, as Attewell (2001) demonstrates. Highly selective "star" high schools may not serve their middle- and lower-achieving students as well as if they were enrolled in a less selective school.

Again, an example from New York is instructive. *The Directory of the Public High Schools, 2002–2003*, distributed to eighth and ninth graders in the New York City, is almost 500 pages in length and contains information about 230 New York City high schools. Students and their parents may apply to a number of schools (and even more programs!) across the city and within their own boroughs, and are guaranteed a place in a school in whose zone they reside. The directory is modeled after the college guides that are so prominent in the college admissions process. While all schools are required to offer a curriculum that prepares students for the Regents examinations, the settings in which that education is offered vary tremendously in size, focus, fellow students, extra- and co-curricular offerings, and just about all other aspects as well. No one would argue against providing such information to parents, in English and Spanish (and abridged versions in Chinese, Haitian Creole, Russian, and Korean), but the necessary knowledge and judgment to use that information effectively is not necessarily available in all families.

The important legacy of the comprehensive high school for us today, I believe, is its commitment, even if only rarely achieved, to provide an education to all the youth of a community, and the opportunity for them to get to know and interact with each other. This is a very rare aspiration and reality today, as secondary schools are more segregated by race and class than ever (Orfield, with Gordon, 2001). Indeed, some are now calling for "mixed classes" as a means of improving school achievement (Kahlenberg, 2000). Asserting that access to a school that middle-class parents would want for their children should be a right of all children, Kahlenberg describes two districts that redistricted their schools to more evenly divide their youth among schools. This policy had the effect of raising the achievement levels of low-performing youth while sustaining that of highly performing youth. While the rationale for this change is often the desire to reduce "the learning gap," it has also eliminated a source of division and resentment in the communities and helped to better prepare all the youth for life in a democratic and very diverse society. More recently, Cambridge, Massachusetts, and San Francisco, California, have adopted similar plans (Marlantes, 2001; Rimer, 2003).

The wide variation in individual accomplishments before entering high school poses the greatest threat to high school reform efforts. Recognizing that the obligation of public education is to promote social mobility, educators and policymakers have embarked on an effort to deliver on the promise of education in our society. The great variety and inequality of family environments from which these students come, however, generate anew the differences in student readiness for high school and is the greatest and most enduring reality against which we must struggle. To offer a secondary program appropriate for *all* our youth is the challenge.

WHAT ABOUT JAMES B. CONANT?

Conant did not invent the comprehensive high school. It had been around for more than 50 years when his book came out. He did solidify its place in U.S. education, however, at a time of rising criticism. The new forms of high schools are still evolving, and there is much flux today in high school organization. The fate of the senior year, for example, is being questioned, at least for those doing well academically. As I described in Chapter 1, the blending of the secondary and postsecondary sectors is evident at the same time that we are trying to raise the overall standards for everyone. High school attainment is not becoming more equal, but through AP classes, dual enrollment plans and early college high schools, it is blending, at its upper reaches, into college.

The comprehensive high school was the dominant organizational form for public secondary education in the United States for almost 100 years, through the 20th century. In many communities, especially in well-to-do suburban areas and many small towns, it remains strong. The combination of academic and community service functions, cultural and athletic activities, and links to local businesses through coop education and school-to-work programs makes the comprehensive high school a very central part of many communities. In poor urban neighborhoods, its size and outward emphasis—to college and the professional worlds—seems to many students misplaced and alien. For many, the train out of town that Driscoll describes in Chapter 6 never leaves the station. It is particularly in these locations, also discussed in Rury's Chapter 3, that the challenges to comprehensiveness have had the greatest impact. Although ongoing, the urban high school revolution has swept many large comprehensive high schools into the dustbin of history, where they may well remain.

I do not think it fair to sweep Conant there as well. Conant would have been dismayed by the great expansion of college enrollments that has been the most important death knell to the comprehensive high school. He complained in some detail about the overly ambitious suburban parents who wanted their not so academically adept children to get into college, and into "good" colleges. He did not think college was for all, and could be seen as trying to protect the eliteness of postsecondary institutions by fostering general and vocational education in high schools.

The enormous expansion of postsecondary enrollments (Brown, 1995; Collins, 1979; Labaree, 1996) was fueled by a combination of the baby boom and our relentless use of educational credentials to ration access to desirable jobs. Conant's message in 1959, that the comprehensive high school model was still relevant and that only small, incremental changes were necessary, was reassuring and widely endorsed. It is well to remember that *Sputnik* was lofted by the Soviet Union in 1957, Fidel Castro's revolution won Cuba in 1958, Khrushchev had threatened Berlin, and the mainland Chinese were eyeing the Nationalist Chinese-occupied islands of Quemoy and Matsu. Conant was a "cold warrior," having been High Commissioner to Germany and then ambassador after leaving Harvard's presidency in 1953. But he was always aware of what set the United States apart from the Soviet bloc (Preskill, 1998). His focus on the social as well as academic purpose of high schools was strongly influenced by his sense of the threat from the Soviet Union and its allies.

Praise for Conant's work was not universal, but it was 20 years before significant criticism of the comprehensive high school model began with the *Nation at Risk* report of 1983. This was quickly followed by Boyer (1983), Sizer (1984), and Powell, Farrar, and Cohen (1985), who reiterated the "lack of rigor" critique that helped spawn the standards reform movement of today. This was long after the red scare had dissipated.

CONCLUSIONS

The key problems of secondary education that the comprehensive high school was created to address remain with us today. Reflecting back on the intentions as well as the actions of its inventors is useful now because we face the same issues, even though the context in which they play out is quite different. There are dilemmas or, perhaps better, contradictions embedded in our secondary education efforts. We seek to offer individual and communal benefits; we seek to encourage excellence among individuals but also to assure a minimum level of achievement for all; we seek to assure equal opportunity, but within a system in which there are vast inequalities among the participants; and we use education to justify differential rewards, but often blunt merit through unearned privileges. These societal and cultural contradictions motivate our efforts at educational reform even as they frustrate its achievement.

In our efforts to create more academically effective schools, we need to guard against undermining our ability to foster community solidarity and integration. As we experiment with new organizational forms for secondary education and new expectations for all students, we need to remain alert to the potential to inadvertently reinforce the inequalities we seek to overcome. While the comprehensive high school never fully realized its promise, we can benefit from an understanding of its successes and failures to provide an education for all of a community's youth. We face the same issues today as we attempt to provide a college preparatory education to all of our youth.

REFERENCES

Angus, D. L., & Mirel, J. E. (1999). *The failed promise of the American high school, 1890–1995*. New York: Teachers College Press.

Attewell, P. (2001). The winner-take-all high school: Organizational adaptations to educational stratification. *Sociology of Education, 74*(4), 267–295.

Boas, K. (2002, August 21). The latest essential for college applicants: A summer already spent on campus. *The New York Times*, p. B8.

Bottoms, G., Presson, A., & Johnson, M. (1992). *Making high schools work through integration of academic and vocational education*. Atlanta: Southern Regional Education Board.

Boyer, E. L. (1983). *High school: A report of the Carnegie Foundation for the advancement of teaching*. New York: Harper & Row.

Brown, D. K. (1995). *Degrees of control: A sociology of educational expansion and occupational credentialism*. New York: Teachers College Press.

Cobb, C. D., & Glass, G. V. (1999). Ethnic segregation in Arizona charter schools. *Education Policy Analysis Archives, 7*(1) (January 14, 1999). http://epaa.asu.edu/epaa/v7n1/

Cohen, E. G., & Lotan, R. A. (Eds.). (1997). *Working for equity in heterogeneous classrooms: Sociological theory in practice*. New York: Teachers College Press.

Collins, R. (1979). *The credential society: An historical sociology of education and stratification.* Orlando: Academic Press.

Commission on the Reorganization of Secondary Education. (1918). *Cardinal principles of secondary education.* Washington, D.C.: U.S. Bureau of Education, Bulletin No. 35.

Croninger, R. G., Johnson, D. J., & Bodone, F. (2000). *Schools-within-schools: A high school reform for what and for whom?* Paper presented at the annual meeting of the American Educational Research Association, New Orleans.

Dougherty, K. J. (1997). Mass higher education: What is its impetus? What is its impact? *Teachers College Record 99*(1), 66–72.

Gamoran, A. (2000). High standards: A strategy for equalizing opportunities to learn? In R. D. Kahlenberg (Ed.), *A notion at risk: Preserving public education as an engine for social mobility* (pp. 93–126). New York: The Century Foundation/Twentieth Century Fund.

Gamoran, A., Porter, A. C., Smithson, J., & White, P. A. (1997). Upgrading high school mathematics instruction: Improving learning opportunities for low-income, low-achieving youth. *Educational Evaluation and Policy Analysis, 19*(4), 325–338.

Gehring, J. (2001a). The international baccalaureate: "Cadillac" of college-prep programs. *Education Week, 20*(32), 19.

Gehring, J. (2001b). Dual-enrollment programs spreading. *Education Week, 20*(32), 17–18.

Goldin, C. (1998). America's graduation from high school: The evolution and spread of secondary schooling in the twentieth century. *Journal of Economic History, 57,* 345–374.

Hartocollis, A. (2001, February 28). High school drop out rate rises, and Levy fears new test will bring huge surge. *The New York Times,* p. B6.

Kahlenberg, R. D. (2000). Mixing classes: Why economic desegregation holds the key to school reform. *The Washington Monthly Online.* December. www.washingtonmonthly.com/features/2000/0012.kahlenberg.html

Kahlenberg, R. D. (2001). *All together now: Creating middle-class schools through public school choice.* Washington, D.C.: Brookings Institution Press.

Krug, E. A. (1972). *The shaping of the American high school: Vol. 2. 1920–1941.* Madison: University of Wisconsin Press.

Labaree, D. F. (1988). *The making of an American high school: The credentials market and Central High School of Philadelphia, 1838–1939.* New Haven: Yale University Press.

Labaree, D. F. (1996). Public goods, private goods: The American struggle over educational goals. *American Educational Research Journal, 34*(1), 39–81.

Lee, V. E., Croninger, R. G., & Smith, J. B. (1996). Equity and choice in Detroit. In B. Fuller & R. E. Elmore (Eds.), *Who chooses? Who loses?* (pp. 70–91). New York: Teachers College Press.

Legters, N. E., Balfanz, R., Jordan, W. J., & McPartland, J. M. (2002). *Comprehensive reform for urban high schools: A talent development approach.* New York: Teachers College Press.

Levine, D. U. (1966). Whatever happened to the ideal of the comprehensive school? *Phi Delta Kappan, 48*(2), 62–64.

Lewin, T. (2002, February, 22). Harvard to require top score to earn advanced placement. *The New York Times*, p. A20.

Lucas, S. R. (1999). *Tracking inequality: Stratification and mobility in American high schools.* New York: Teachers College Press.

Mann, H. (1976, originally published 1848). Report for 1848: Intellectual education as a means of removing poverty, and securing abundance. In Henry J. Perkinson (Ed.), *Two hundred years of American educational thought* (pp. 80–102). New York: McKay.

Marlantes, L. (2001). Schools now integrate by income. *Christian Science Monitor*, December 20. http://www.csmonitor.com/2001/1220/p1s1-usgn.html.

Metz, M. H. (2003). *Different by design: The context and character of three magnet schools* (reissued with a new introduction). New York: Teachers College Press.

National Center for Educational Statistics. (1997). *Digest of educational statistics.* Washington, D.C.: U.S. Department of Education. http://www.nces.ed.gov/edstats/digest97/d97t378.html.

National Educational Association. (1894). *Report of the Committee of Ten on secondary school studies.* New York: American Book Co.

Oakes, J. (1992). Can tracking research inform practice? Technical, normative and political considerations. *Educational Researcher, 21*(4), 12–22.

Orfield, G., with Gordon, N. (2001). *Schools more separate: Consequences of a decade of resegregation.* Cambridge, MA: Civil Rights Project, Harvard University. http://www.law.harvard.edu/civilrights/publications/pressseg.html

Powell, A. G., Farrar, E., & Cohen, D. K. (1985). *The shopping mall high school: Winners and losers in the educational marketplace.* Boston: Houghton Mifflin.

Preskill, S. (1998). National school reform: The early cold war era. In S. E. Tozer, P. C. Violas, & G. Senese (Eds.), *School and society: Historical and contemporary perspectives* (pp. 217–241). New York: McGraw-Hill.

Ready, D. D., Lee, V. E., & LoGerfo, L. F. (2000). *Social and academic stratification in high schools divided into schools-within-schools.* Paper read at the 2000 annual meetings of the American Educational Research Association, New Orleans, LA.

Resnick, L. B. (1999). Foreword. In D. D. Marsh, J. B. Codding & Associates, *The new American high school* (pp. vii–xvi). Thousand Oaks, CA: Corwin.

Rimer, S. (2003, May 8). Schools try integration by income, not race. *New York Times*, A1.

Rosenbaum, J. E. (2001). *Beyond college for all.* New York: Russell Sage Foundation.

Rothstein, R. (2002, October 9). Dropout rate is climbing and likely to go higher. *The New York Times*, B8.

Rubenstein, R. C. 2001. *The future of high school reform: The emerging consensus.* [Paper]: Washington, D.C.: National Commission on the High School Senior Year. [on-line]: http://commissiononthesenioryear.org/Suggested_Reading/thefuture.html

Sizer, T. R. (1984). *Horace's compromise: The dilemma of the American high school.* Boston: Houghton Mifflin.

Trow, M. (1961). The second transformation of American secondary education. *International Journal of Comparative Sociology, 2*(2), 144–166.

Ueda, R. (1994). *Avenues to adulthood: The origins of the high school and social mobility in an American suburb.* New York: Cambridge University Press.

Viadero, D. (2001, April 25). AP program assumes larger role. *Education Week,* 1, 16, 18, 19. http://www.edweek.com/ew/ew_printstory.cfm?slug=32ap.h20

Wilensky, R. (2001, May 9). Wrong, wrong, wrong. *Education Week, 20*(34), 48, 32.

About the Editor and Contributors

Floyd M. Hammack is Associate Professor of Educational Sociology and Higher Education at New York University's Steinhardt School of Education. He studies the connections among and between secondary schools and higher education. His B.A. and M.A. are from the University of Oregon, and his Ph.D. in sociology is from Florida State University. He is the editor (with Kevin Dougherty) of *Education and Society: A Reader* (1990). His most recent article, "The Channeling of Student Competition in Higher Education" (with Scott Davies), will appear *in The Journal of Higher Education.*

Mary Erina Driscoll is associate professor and director of the program in Educational Administration in the Steinhardt School of Education at New York University. A graduate of Connecticut College, her M.A. is from Sarah Lawrence college and her Ph.D. is from the University of Chicago. Her research focuses on the connections between schools and their communities and, most recently, on the ways in which communities can serve as contexts for student learning. Dr. Driscoll has served as president of the University Council for Educational Administration and has been active in the National Policy Board for Educational Administration. A recent publication is "The sense of place and the neighborhood school: Implications for Building Social Capital and for Community Development," in R. Crowson (Ed.), *Community Development and School Reform* (2001).

Joseph P. McDonald is professor of Teaching and Learning at New York University's Steinhardt School of Education. A graduate of the University of Scranton, his M.A.T. and Ed.D. degrees are from Harvard's Graduate School of Education. His most recent book is *The Power of Protocols* (2003). Other of his books that deal with high school are *School Reform Behind the Scenes* (1999), *Redesigning School* (1996), and *Teaching: Making Sense of an Uncertain Craft* (1992). His current research projects include a study of the scaling-up of a new high school design, as well as a study of school reform in four large American cities. He is a former high school teacher and principal.

Jeannie Oakes is Presidential Professor in Educational Equity and Director of UCLA's Institute for Democracy, Education & Access (IDEA) and the University of California's All Campus Consortium on Research for Diversity (ACCORD). Dr. Oakes's research examines inequalities in U.S. schools and follows the progress of equity-minded reform. She is the author of 17 scholarly books and monographs and more than 100 published research reports, chapters, and articles, including *Keeping Track: How Schools Structure Inequality* (1985). Her latest book is *Becoming Good American Schools: The Struggle for Civic Virtue in Education Reform* (2000), with Karen Hunter Quartz, Steve Ryan, and Martin Lipton.

John L. Rury is professor and chair, Department of Teaching and Leadership, University of Kansas. His A.B. is from Fordham, his M.S.Ed. is from the City University of New York, and his Ph.D. is from the University of Wisconsin. He is a social historian who studies education, urban development, and social inequality. His books include *Education and Social Change* (2002), *Education and Women's Work* (1991), and *Seeds of Crisis: Public Schooling in Milwaukee Since 1920* (1993). Additional publications have appeared in *History of Education Quarterly*, *Social Science History*, *Teachers College Record*, the *Journal of Negro Education*, *Educational Policy*, and other journals. From 1992 to 1996 he served as editor of the Social and Institutional Analysis section of the *American Educational Research Journal*, and from 1999 to 2002 he was a senior program Officer at the Spencer Foundation.

Roger Shouse, associate professor of Education at The Pennsylvania State University, is a graduate of the University of Chicago Department of Education and a former Spencer Post-Doctoral Fellow. His scholarship has spanned an array of education topics including school culture, student achievement, and curricular reform. His current work highlights the informal, semistructured aspects of school life and how these contribute to students' moral learning. Shouse has authored or co-authored such articles as "Academic Press, Sense of Community: Conflict and Congruence in American High Schools" (*Research in Sociology of Education and Socialization*, 11) and "School Restructuring as Policy Agenda: Why One Size May Not Fit All" (*Sociology of Education*, 74:1).

Amy Stuart Wells is a professor of Sociology and Education at Teachers College, Columbia University. Her research and writing have focused broadly on issues of race and education and more specifically on educational policies such as school desegregation, school choice, charter schools, and tracking and how they shape and constrain opportunities for students of color. She is the author and editor of *Where Charter School Policy Fails: The Problems of Accountability and Equity* (2002); co-author with Robert L. Crain of *Stepping over the Color Line: African American Students in White Suburban Schools* (1997); co-editor with A. H. Halsey, Hugh Lauder, and Phillip Brown of *Education: Culture, Economy and Society* (1997); and co-author with Irene Serna of "The Politics of Culture: Understanding Local Political Resistance to Detracking in Racially Mixed Schools," *Harvard Educational Review*, Spring 1996.

Index